实用商务英语写作

主　编　李　蓉　胡　金　蒋　霞
副主编　谭　英　唐日芳　彭奉天
　　　　阳有明　亢江瑶

清华大学出版社
北京交通大学出版社
·北京·

内 容 简 介

《实用商务英语写作》从国际商务实际出发，以国际贸易流程为主线，将国际商务知识与英语融于一体，旨在帮助学生熟悉国际商务和外贸的各个环节，能与客户进行有效的沟通。本书首先介绍商务写作的定义和作用，然后通过遴选地道的美国商界最新范例介绍备忘录、商务便条、商务报告、商业建议书等常用商务文体，再逐一展现贸易实践各环节使用的函电，涵盖建立业务关系、询价、报盘、还盘、订货、支付、包装、装运、保险、索赔等各个环节，系统地介绍外贸英语函电的专业用语、写作特点及技巧，并通过理论联系实际的方法，训练学生正确使用信函中常用的句型和词汇，达到熟练地翻译和撰写业务信函的目的。

本书适合高等院校经贸方向的学生使用，也适合有志于从事国际贸易的人士参考使用。

本书封面贴有清华大学出版社防伪标签，无标签者不得销售。
版权所有，侵权必究。侵权举报电话：010 –62782989 13501256678 13801310933

图书在版编目（CIP）数据

实用商务英语写作 / 李蓉，胡金，蒋霞主编 . — 北京：北京交通大学出版社：清华大学出版社，2017.9（2020.1 重印）

ISBN 978-7-5121-3324-2

Ⅰ．①实… Ⅱ．①李… ②胡… ③蒋… Ⅲ．①商务－英语－写作 Ⅳ．①F7

中国版本图书馆 CIP 数据核字（2017）第 192702 号

实用商务英语写作
SHIYONG SHANGWU YINGYU XIEZUO

责任编辑：孙晓萌
出版发行：清 华 大 学 出 版 社　　邮编：100084　　电话：010-62776969　　http://www.tup.com.cn
　　　　　北京交通大学出版社　　邮编：100044　　电话：010-51686414　　http://www.bjtup.com.cn
印 刷 者：北京鑫海金澳胶印有限公司
经　　销：全国新华书店
开　　本：185 mm×260 mm　　印张：16　　字数：399 千字
版　　次：2017 年 9 月第 1 版　　2020 年 1 月第 2 次印刷
书　　号：ISBN 978-7-5121-3324-2/F·1716
定　　价：39.00 元

本书如有质量问题，请向北京交通大学出版社质监组反映。对您的意见和批评，我们表示欢迎和感谢。
投诉电话：010-51686043，51686008；传真：010-62225406；E-mail：press@bjtu.edu.cn。

前　言

商务写作在涉外经济活动中具有联络业务、沟通交流的作用，对市场的开拓和贸易的发展具有积极作用。《实用商务英语写作》从国际商务实际出发，以国际贸易流程为主线，将国际商务知识与英语融于一体，旨在帮助学生熟悉国际商务和外贸的各个环节，能与客户进行有效的沟通。本书首先介绍商务写作的定义和作用，然后通过遴选地道的美国商界最新范例介绍备忘录、商务便条、商务报告、商业建议书等常用商务文体，再逐一展现贸易实践各环节使用的函电，涵盖建立业务关系、询价、报盘、还盘、订货、支付、包装、装运、保险、索赔等各个环节，系统地介绍外贸英语函电的专业用语、写作特点及技巧，并通过理论联系实际的方法，训练学生正确使用信函中常用的句型和词汇，达到熟练地翻译和撰写业务信函的目的。

全书共分为4个部分。第一部分系统介绍商务写作的基本知识；第二部分介绍常用商务写作文体，如备忘录、商务便条、商务报告、商业建议书等，遴选地道的美国商界商务范文，结合范文和即时练习，为学生学习各类商务写作文体提供帮助；第三部分以外贸函电为主，由易渐难地从寻找客户、磋商订单、签订合同、处理纠纷和寻找代理等方面逐一展现外贸的各个环节，介绍了建立业务关系、询价、报盘、还盘、订货、支付、包装、装运、保险、索赔、代理等内容；第四部分为实训部分，通过案例的方式让学生完成贸易中整套信函的撰写。

本书的编写遵循立体化和信息化的原则。①立体化。除文本外，教材内容还通过声音、图像、图形、表格、图媒体等信息符号呈现，同时将教材制作成APK、ePub电子书，学生可通过手机、平板电脑等便携式终端浏览，增强学生的学习兴趣，适应学生的个性化学习要求。②信息化。"互联网+"环境下，屏幕越来越占据主导地位，移动学习已成为不可或缺的学习方式之一，鼓励和支持学生带手机进入课堂的呼声越来越高。二维码是移动互联网和O2O的关键入口，教材编写中引入二维码技术突破了时空的限制，通过二维码连接教材与网络世界，所包含的教学内容与网络富媒体资源互传、互补，实现共享。码书,"纸质教材+二维码+手机"形成重要的互动网络化学习内容,学生掏出手机"扫一扫",内容可以是一段音频、视频,也可以是课后习题的答案或反馈式交互测验等。将二维码嵌入教材是教材的一种大胆的尝试,也是本次教材修订最主要的特色之一。二维码可以强化知识信息的传播,使课内知识与课外知识的交融更加充分、自如。此外,本书充分利用现代教育技术手段的技术先进、信息量大、使用便捷、形式新奇等特性,在内容和表现形式上体现多样性、生动性和互动性。本书把外贸函电与相关的国际贸易实务课程的内容有机地衔接起来,在内容的编排上充分体现以学生为中心的原则,向学生展现真实的外贸业务环节,诱发学生的学习兴趣,激发学生的学习主动性,特别是实训部分的贸易单证为实践教学提供了相应的素材,便于学生将学习与实习、就业联系起来,充分调动学生学习的积极性和参与性。本书适合高等院校经贸方向的学生使用,也适合有志于从事国际贸易的人士参考使用。

本书由桂林理工大学教材建设基金和外国语学院资助出版,是 2015 年广西高等教育本科教学改革工程项目一般 B 类"基于可理解性输入和输出理论的商务英语'三多'教学模式研究与实践"的阶段性成果,也是桂林理工大学外国语学院 2016 年强基项目优势特色专业(英语专业)的建设成果。本书由桂林理工大学外国语学院李蓉、胡金、蒋霞担任主编,桂林理工大学外国语学院谭英、唐日芳、彭奉天、现教中心阳有明担任副主编。全书具体的编写分工为:彭奉天负责编写第 1～2 章;唐日芳负责编写第 3 章和第 17 章;谭英负责编写第 4～6 章和第 18～20 章;李蓉、蒋霞负责编写第 7～16 章;李蓉、胡金、尤江瑶负责所有资源的收集和编辑,阳有明负责后期电子资源的制作与编辑。

为答谢广大教师对本书的厚爱,编者特向选用本书的教师免费提供每章练习的参考答案,有需要的教师可发邮件至编者的邮箱 1714311379@qq.com 索取。

由于编者水平有限,书中疏漏之处在所难免,敬请广大读者赐教指正。

编 者
2017 年 9 月

目 录

Part 1　An Overview of Business Writing ……………… 1
　Chapter 1　Definition and Function of Business Writing ……………… 2
　Chapter 2　Fundamentals of Effective Business Writing ……………… 5

Part 2　Major Business Writing ……………………… 11
　Chapter 3　Business E-mail ……………………………… 12
　Chapter 4　Business Memo ……………………………… 26
　Chapter 5　Business Report ……………………………… 36
　Chapter 6　Business Proposal …………………………… 58
　Chapter 7　Business Letter ……………………………… 73

Part 3　Routine Business Transaction Letter …………… 87
　Chapter 8　Inquiry and Reply …………………………… 88
　Chapter 9　Price Discussion ……………………………… 99
　Chapter 10　Order and Reply …………………………… 113
　Chapter 11　Payment …………………………………… 124
　Chapter 12　Packing …………………………………… 136
　Chapter 13　Shipping …………………………………… 147
　Chapter 14　Insurance …………………………………… 159
　Chapter 15　Complaint and Settlement ………………… 170
　Chapter 16　Business Partnership ……………………… 184

Part 4　Simulation Training in Business Writing ·············· 203
　　Chapter 17　Business Correspondence ·············· 204
　　Chapter 18　Business Memo Writing ·············· 243
　　Chapter 19　Business Report Writing ·············· 245
　　Chapter 20　Business Proposal Writing ·············· 247

参考文献·············· 250

Part 1

An Overview of Business Writing

扫描二维码　阅读了解
"Difference Between Academic Writing and Business Writing"

扫描二维码　阅读了解
"How Is Business Writing Different from Academic Writing"

Chapter 1

Definition and Function of Business Writing

> **Brainstorm**
>
> (1) How to define business writing? What's the difference between business writing and other writings?
> (2) Why is business writing important?

扫描二维码
浏览视频
"Why Is Business Writing Important"

The term business writing refers to all bodies of text which have to do with the description or dealings of business—examples of these are business letters, memos, E-mails, proposals, resumes, cover letters as well as the texts in brochures and other forms of company advertisements.

Business writing is one of the most important aspects of the business world. Writing is still one of the number one methods of communication in the world. With the introduction of E-mail, writing became even more important in the work place. There are many different types of business writing. Each type is designed to work toward a different goal. Being aware of the different types of business writing and also being able to write in several different business styles will help a person become a great business communicator.

Generally speaking, correspondence, including letters, E-mails, newsgroups, Internet forums, blogs, etc., refers to non-concurrent, remote communication through exchange of letters between people. A Businessperson writes and receives letters in his or her day-to-day transactions, which may be called business correspondence. Business correspondence or business letter is a written communication between two parties for achieving specific business objectives. For example, a businessperson may write letters to the supplier of goods and also receive letters from the suppliers; on the other hand, a customer may write letters to a businessperson for seeking information about availability of goods, price, quality, sample, etc. or placing an order for purchase of goods.

Business writing has been around as long as business and writing. Thousands of years ago business people kept track of transactions and inventory through writing.

Chapter 1 Definition and Function of Business Writing

As more international business became usual, business letters became a huge aspect of the business world. After the invention of the phone business, writing became less common, however, when E-mail became popular for business use, business writing again became a very necessary part of the business world.

Business writing is very important because it is one of the number one ways that people are viewed professionally. If someone has a sloppy writing style, then he will be seen as a sloppy person. People who can communicate clearly through writing in the business world will have a higher chance of receiving promotions and job offers. It is also important that business writing be done in a clear and concise manner so that the recipients of the writing can actually understand the point of the writing.

Nowadays business operations are not restricted to any locality, state or nation because production takes place in one area while consumption takes place everywhere. Thus, business writing should be promotional, motivational, informational, and persuasive.

1. Maintain Proper Relationship

Business activities are not confined to any one area or locality in the modern society, as the businessmen and customers are scattered throughout the country. Thus, there is a need to maintain proper relationship among them by using appropriate, economical and convenient means of communication. In this case, business letters play an important role, in which the customers can write to the businessperson seeking information about products and the businessperson in turn can supply various information to customers. This helps them to carry on business on national and international basis economically and conveniently.

2. Create and Maintain Goodwill

The message contained in the business letters will exert certain impact on the readers. The professional and appropriate expressions and writing skills reflected in business letters might give readers good impression and thus arouse their trust in the products and service of a company. This might be really valuable for the success of a deal.

3. Serve as Evidence

It is impossible for a trader to memorize all facts and figures in a conversation that normally takes place among businesspersons. Through letters, he can keep a record of all facts for organizing the transactions of the international trade. Thus, letters can also serve as evidence in case of dispute between two parties.

4. Expand Business

Business letters are used to convey a vast amount of information regarding competing products, prevailing prices, promotions, market activities, etc. so as to complete day-to-day business operations. If the trader has to run from place to place to get information, it will simply result in loss of time. But through business letters, he can make all inquiries about the products and the markets. He can also receive orders from different countries and, thus enhance sales.

Exercises

I. Fill in the blanks.

1. Business letters serve as a/an _____ in case of dispute in business transactions.
2. It is _____ for the businessmen to remember all facts without correspondence.
3. Thousands of years ago business people kept track of _____ and _____ through writing.
4. Business writing should be promotional, motivational, informational, and _____.
5. Business letters are used to convey _____ regarding competing products, prevailing prices, promotions, market activities, etc.

II. Write "T" for true statements and "F" for false statements.

1. A letter is a form of written communication. ( )
2. Through business letters, personal contact can be maintained between buyer and seller. ( )
3. Business letters lead people to the decline of the goodwill of the firm. ( )
4. A letter is a convenient and economic mode of communication. ( )
5. Business letters do not help in removing misunderstanding between buyer and seller. ( )

Chapter 2

Fundamentals of Effective Business Writing

> **Brainstorm**
>
> (1) Are you an experienced writer? Do you often write in plain and simple language?
> (2) Why is it that "A message aimed at everyone often appeals to no one"?

We're bombarded with words, all day, every day—E-mails, brochures, reports, letters, ads, speeches, articles, PowerPoint presentations, etc.

You can't afford to let your business communications get lost in the crowd—not if you want to inspire your customers to buy, encourage your employees to work harder, or simply invite associates to a business luncheon.

Here are a few ways to make your writings stand out from the pack.

扫描二维码
浏览视频
"The ABCs of Business Writing"

1. Know Your Audience

It's an old saying in the advertising business: A message aimed at everyone often appeals to no one.

To communicate effectively, you have to know your readers. Are they familiar with your subject? Are they likely to resist your message? Are they old or young, urban or rural, highly educated or not?

Knowing your readers makes it easier for you to answer everyone's most pressing question, "What's in it for me?"

> **Tip:** Picture the typical reader in your mind. Is he or she a 18-year-old university student from a small town or a 60-year-old executive in a big city?

2. Know Your Message

Before typing a word, decide what you're trying to achieve. Do you simply want to share information? Do you need to explain a difficult concept? Or do you want to inspire your readers to act? Most importantly, what is your key message?

> **Tip:** Try to boil your message down to an ad-style slogan—for instance, "This product can save your business thousands of dollars a year."

3. Think like a Reporter

When you're closely involved with a topic, it's easy to overlook the obvious. For example, it's astonishing how many websites for hotels and restaurants don't include one vital piece of information: the address. Make sure your document includes the answers to 5 W's and 1 H: who, what, where, when, why and how.

> **Tip:** Show your document to someone outside your department or company and ask whether anything is missing.

4. Banish Buzzwords and Cliches

Too much business writing these days is stuffed with cliches and over-used buzzwords. What business isn't "service-oriented"? And if a company isn't "solutions-focused", what is it focused on? Creating problems?

Cliches are expressions that come out of nowhere and suddenly seem to be everywhere, to the point that they become almost meaningless. How many times have you read about terms like "win-win solutions" or "time is money"? Do they inspire you or make you yawn?

> **Tip:** When you detect a cliche, try to come up with a fresher metaphor for the same idea. Instead of "thinking outside the box", how about "breaking away from the herd"? But don't work too hard to be clever. Often, simply saying what you mean—"thinking in innovative ways" is best.

5. Junk the Jargon

Every field has its acronyms and technical terms. They're useful shorthand when every reader knows the lingo. But if you're writing for people outside your field—which will often include your customers—get rid of the inside slang or you may create confusion.

> **Tip:** If you absolutely can't avoid using jargon, at least explain it. On a webpage, for instance, you can insert a hyperlink to the definition.

6. Keep It Tight

Short sentences, short paragraphs and short documents have a better chance of capturing readers' attention. That's particularly true of E-mails and other electronic documents because we read more slowly on screen than on paper. Here are a few tips.

Delete redundant adjectives. All friends are personal; all innovations are new; all disasters are serious.

Don't disguise your verbs as verb/noun pairs. Don't "make a decision" or "carry out an improvement". Just "decide" or "improve."

Cut windy phrases. Why say "We are in the process of upgrading our IT systems" when you can simply say "We are upgrading our IT systems"?

> **Tip:** Pretend the document you're working on is a telegram and every word costs you $10. Edit accordingly.

7. Make It Plain and Simple

People often skim documents for key information before deciding to read the whole thing. Make it easy for them.

Write a clear subject line for your E-mail or a clear headline for your article.

Put deadlines and other vital points in bold.

Break up messages with descriptive subheads.

Put lists—like this one—in bullet format.

Make sure the most important information is at the top.

And avoid using $20 words when 20-cent ones will do. Instead of "facilitating ameliorations to our customer service environment", simply "improve customer service".

> **Tip:** Try to write like you speak.

8. Leave the Symbols and Abbreviations on Your Phone

When you're writing to your kids, go ahead and use "&" "etc." "e.g." and other shorthand. But if you're writing to impress clients, employees or investors, use full words. It's simply more professional.

> **Tip:** If you frequently use certain symbols, put a sticky note on your computer monitor reminding yourself to "search and replace" them.

9. Get Active

What's the difference between these two sentences?

"Rebates will be provided on all new purchases."

"XYZ Corp. will provide rebates on all new purchases."

In the first case, we don't know who is providing the rebate. In the second, the company is the subject of the sentence.

In grammatical terms, the first sentence is in the passive voice and the second is in the active voice. But why should you care? Putting sentences in active voice is a quick way to brighten your writing. Sentences in active voice are often shorter and usually clearer than those in passive voice, and inspire more trust in readers. Everyone wants to know who is doing what.

> **Tip:** Ask yourself "Who is acting in this sentence?" If that person or organization isn't in the sentence, add it as the subject of the verb.

10. Proofread

Spell checkers are useful tools, but they're far from perfect. They'll rarely alert you when you've used an actual word in the wrong context—just ask anyone who has ever invited customers to contact the "sales manger". Proofread your documents before printing them or hitting "send".

> **Tip:** Read documents aloud to catch missing words. And if you see one mistake, read the rest of the paragraph particularly closely.

Exercises

I. Write "T" for true statements and "F" for false statements.

1. Knowing your readers makes no difference for you to write effectively. ( )
2. Cliches are expressions that people use over and over again thus are considered vital parts in business writing. ( )
3. If you're writing to people outside your field, you'd better do not use jargon which is hard to comprehend. ( )
4. Short sentences, short paragraphs and short documents are more welcome by readers. ( )
5. Instead of using plain and simple language, long and complex sentences are more encouraged in business writing. ( )
6. Active voice is often shorter and usually clearer than passive voice, and inspires more trust in readers. ( )

II. Change the following sentences into active voice.

Arrangements have been made for a repeat order to be dispatched to you today.
_____

The cause of your complaint has been investigated.
_____

The seminar will be conducted by Adrian Chan.
_____

A workshop will be held next Tuesday and all members of the board are required to attend the meeting.
_____
_____

Part 2

Major Business Writing

扫描二维码 阅读了解
"Forms of Business Writing"

扫描二维码 阅读了解
"Types of Written Business Communication"

扫描二维码 阅读了解
"Types of Communication in Business Writing"

Chapter 3

Business E-mail

Brainstorm

(1) What is E-mail?
(2) What is the format of E-mail?
(3) What should be paid attention to in writing business E-mails?

1. Introduction

E-mail, short for electronic mail, is the transmission of messages over communication networks. E-mail can be done for both personal and business communications. Users of E-mail can send or reply to a message, forward a message (send a received E-mail message to another person or other persons), save a message (save or download an E-mail message onto disc), or trash a message (delete an E-mail message which the user doesn't want to keep). E-mail can include words, pictures, sounds and video clips.

Nowadays, E-mail has been widely used and is playing an increasingly important role in business communication as a fast, economical and efficient means. In the business world, E-mails are widely used in both internal and external communications for consultation, action, material supply, suggestion, warning, solution and other business purposes. In the former case, it may be interoffice messages between colleagues; in the latter, it may be between business firms and customers, or between firms and suppliers.

2. Format of E-mail

An E-mail is sometimes sent and replied by the receiver later, but sometimes it is possible to communicate or "talk" online if both users are connected to the modem at the same time. However, in most cases, an E-mail is sent in the form of a letter.

An E-mail normally consists of heading, salutation, body, complimentary close and signature.

1) Heading

Heading usually includes the following elements:

From: The sender's E-mail address.

To: The recipient's E-mail address.

CC (carbon copy): The addresses of different people you want this message sent to.

BCC (blind carbon copy): As with the carbon copy, you can send the same message to someone else. Unlike the CC, the recipients of the message will not know if the same message is sent to only them or also to others.

Subject: The theme or topic of the message, usually very brief.

Attachment: Documents, files, and graphics can be attached.

Date: Date and time automatically appear.

In a business E-mail, the above elements may all appear or partially appear under different circumstances. Normally, the elements including "From" "To" and "Subject" are essential. They can be in the order of "From" "To" and "Subject" or in the order of "To" "From" and "Subject".

2) Salutation

Salutation is the complimentary greeting from the writer. Its form depends on the writer's relationship with the receiver. As to the use of punctuation in the salutation, comma(used in British English) as well as colon (used in American English) is suitable for business E-mail.

Generally speaking, to those you are not familiar with, use formal salutations such as "Dear Mr./ Mrs./Miss/Ms. (last name)", or "Dear (first name)", or "(full name)" flexibly and appropriately.

If you do not know his or her name, it is not wrong to use "To Whom It May Concern" or "Dear Sir or Madam", or use "Dear Sirs" "Dear Madams", or "Gentlemen" for addressing two or more people. But if you know his or her position, it is better to use "Dear (job title)" like "Dear Sales Manager" "Dear HR Director" or "Dear Administrative Assistant", etc..

Such salutations as "Dear (full name)" or "Dear Mr./ Mrs./Miss/Ms. (full name)" are not considered wrong, but they don't fit the habitual use in the business communication.

To those whom you are very familiar with, use informal salutations such as "Dear (first name)" "(first name)" "Hi, (first name)" or "Hello, (first name)" flexibly and appropriately.

It should be noted that, to the same person, a man, for example, your salutations may change with more connection and acquaintance with him. With you becoming business partners, acquaintances and even friends, the salutations may change from "Dear Mr. (last name)" to "Dear (first name)" and to "Hi, (second name)". If you are not sure about that, the safe way is to follow the pattern of the salutation given by the receiver when he replies.

3) Body

In the opening, state directly your purpose of writing or restate or expand the subject line. In the main body, focus on the subject. If you are asking for detailed information, arrange your questions in logical order and rank the important question first. If you are providing information, put similar information into one paragraph. The rule of one paragraph for one idea still dominates. Keep paragraphs short, normally nothing longer than five lines in each paragraph. In the closing, request action, summarize the message or present a closing thought.

4) Complimentary Close

Complimentary close is a polite way of ending an E-mail. The choice of expression depends on the sender's relationship with the receiver. It appears two lines below the last line of the text.

To the superior or older people, use very formal expressions such as "Yours respectfully" (British style), or "Respectfully yours"(American style) .

To the business bosses or associates, use formal expressions like "Yours respectfully" "Yours faithfully" "Yours truly" "Yours gratefully" or "Yours sincerely" flexibly. "Yours sincerely" is a common term for most formal or informal correspondences. If you are not sure about which to use, it is a safe choice in business communication.

"Thank you" (formal) and "Thanks" (casual) are also used in a business setting, especially if you are making a request or asking a question.

"All the best" and "Best wishes" are a polite way to end a letter and it can be used between friends or strangers.

"Best regards" "Warmest regards" "Kindest regards" or "Regards" can be used in daily and business correspondence.

To the acquaintances or friends, use "Yours cordially" "Yours devotedly", or "Yours ever", etc.. To the family members, relatives or close friends, use "Yours affectionately" "Yours lovingly" "Yours ever" "Yours" "Bye for now", or "Yours loving son (daughter, father ,mother…)", etc.. "Take care" is casual and often used between friends.

5) Signature

Formal signature includes name, title/position, company name, address, phone number, and E-mail address. Informal signature is often in the form of first name or diminutive. Here is an example of formal signature.

(electronic handwritten signature)

Lala Du

Manager of Services Department

The National Bank

Add: 199 Songshan Rd., Changsha City, Hunan Province 410003, P. R. China

Tel: 86+ 0731+5558888
E-mail: 123456789@qq.com

3. Guidelines and Tips for Writing Business E-mail

Business E-mail writing should follow the principles of 6 "C", completeness, clarity, concreteness, conciseness, correctness and consideration. A business E-mail can be considered successfully written if it is completely, concisely, concretely, accurately, politely, appropriately and clearly expressed in form and expression in accordance with the etiquette and rules of business correspondence.

1) Identify the Person Whom You Want to Write to

It is important to make a good impression on the recipient. Identifying the person whom you want to write decides what salutations, tones and diction you can use, formal or informal. The level of formality of messages depends on the purpose and the recipient. Therefore, you need to distinguish between formal and informal situations. When you are writing to a friend or a close colleague, it is OK to use "smiles", abbreviations (IIRC for "if I recall recently", LOL for "laughing out loud", etc.) and nonstandard punctuation and spelling (like that found in instant messaging or chat rooms). If you are writing an E-mail message to your customers, suppliers or others, you must carefully organize your message writing, and do use the correct spelling, grammar and format. Always know the situation, and write accordingly.

2) Write a Meaningful and Succinct Subject Line

The subject line of an E-mail should cover only one subject. An informative and succinct subject line can help recipients decide in a short time whether to open, forward, file, or trash a message and thus quicken the handling of the case.

3) Keep the Message Focused, Concise and Readable

E-mail is meant for quick, simple communication. Normally there are roughly four or five paragraphs at most, with each paragraph containing normally nothing longer than six lines. Put your information in the body of your E-mail whenever possible. If it is too long, it is probably best sent as a separate attachment.

Organize the message in an inverted-pyramid structure, with the most important information in the first paragraph.

Try to avoid lines with too complicated structure. If necessary, put numbers before each matter to make the message more understandable; use tables or graphs to break up complicated text; quote from the original E-mail if replying to a message.

4) Don't Flame

To "flame" someone here means to write an abusive personal attack. Never attack your employers, co-workers, customers, or clients. If you find yourself writing in anger, have a break. Take some time to cool off before you hit "send". "Flaming" should not be encouraged in business communication as it will inevitably ruin the business relationship.

Be respectful. Respect shines in writing appropriate salutation and complimentary close, understanding customers' or clients' tradition and customs, and paying attention to their concrete requirements and replying completely and patiently. A potential customer or client can judge just by E-mail whether you and your company are professional, sincere and respectful.

5) Don't Assume Privacy

E-mail is not secure. Don't send anything over E-mail that you wouldn't want posted as it is with your name attached. Do not forward a co-worker's or manager's E-mail without approval. Do not forward confidential or sensitive messages to unintended readers.

6) Check before You Send

After you have finished writing the E-mail, check whether the format is complete, whether it includes the intended information, whether the spelling and the grammar are correct, and whether the word choice and tone are appropriate.

Spelling and grammar still matter in E-mail. Poor spelling and grammar show a lack of attention to detail and send the wrong message about yourself and how you do business. Make sure your messages look professional. If you are not very experienced in writing business letters by E-mail, ask a colleague to read it before it is sent out so as to make sure that your message may not cause any misunderstanding.

7) Respond Promptly

If you want to appear professional and courteous, make yourself available to your online correspondents and respond promptly, and then give your readers reasonable time to respond.

4. Case Study of Business E-mail

Case Study 1: Apology

扫描二维码
浏览视频
"12 Business Writing Tips for Effective Business E-mails and Letters"

From: leslin.miky@tnb.com
To: edward.smith@abc.com
CC: tracy.yun@tnb.com
BCC: dicky. wang@tnb.com
Subject: Apology for Poor Service Rating on Customer Questionnaire

Dear Mr. Smith,

  Thank you for taking time to fill out our questionnaire during your stay with us. We do appreciate hearing from our customers, as their comments are vital for us to continue improving our accommodations.

  The problems that you mentioned have been brought to the attention of our house-keeping department. While the lack of service you experienced is unusual and not the standard of our motel, there is no excuse for a lackadaisical attitude on the part of any of our employees. We are sorry for the inconvenience and annoyance this incident caused.

> Thank you again for your comments. We hope that you will give us another chance to serve you.
>
> Best regards,
Leslin Miky
>
> Leslin Miky (Mr.)
> Manager of Services Department
> The National Bank
> **Add:** 216 Ridgeway St., New Orleans, LA 70170, USA
> **Tel:** (505) 7777-8888
> **E-mail:** leslinmiky@tnb.com

As shown in Case Study 1, this is an E-mail message being sent to the customer. Remember when you write E-mail messages to your customers, suppliers, or other business partners, you need to use the formal business letter format and adopt the appropriate writing tone and diction.

Case Study 2: First Enquiry

> **From:** Mayflower Co. Ltd., Los Angeles
> **To:** Antai Import& Export Co., Beijing
> **ATTN:** Sales Manager
> **Subject:** Enquiry about Your Jute Garments
> **Date:** June 8th, 2016
>
> Dear Sir or Madam,
>
> You are recommended to me by Mr. John of Hi-fashion Garment Ltd. in New York City. Our customer is interested in your 100% jute garments.
>
> Please send me your current price list, an illustrated brochure and the sample jute cloth.
>
> I am looking forward to receiving your reply.
>
> Yours truly,
(signature)
>
> Kim Matthew (Mr.)
> Sales Manager
> Mayflower Co. Ltd., Los Angeles
> **Add:** 405 Hilgard Ave., Los Angeles, CA 90015, USA
> **Tel:** 001+310+8765432
> **E-mail:** kim278@abc.com

Case Study 2 is about the first enquiry between company and company. The message is short, but the format is complete and the information is focused and clearly expressed. "ATTN" is short for "attention". Attention line is used when the writer wishes to direct the letter to a specific individual or section of the firm.

Case Study 3: Reply to the First Enquiry

> **From:** Antai Import& Export Co., Beijing
> **To:** Mayflower Co. Ltd., Los Angeles
> **ATTN:** Sales Manager Mr. Kim Matthew
> **Re:** Your Enquiry Dated June 8th, 2016
> **Date:** June 9th, 2016
>
> Dear Mr. Matthew,
>   We are pleased to send you a price list attached to this E-mail, and an illustrated brochure and the sample jute cloth by EMS separately according to your request.
>   Although we still have certain amount of stock, we can hardly keep them for a long time because of the heavy demand.
>   Your early reply will be appreciated.
>
> Yours Truly,
Betty Yang
>
> Betty Yang (Ms.)
> Sales Manager
> Antai Import& Export Co., Beijing
> **Add:** 133 Xingfu St., Chaoyang District, Beijing 100010, P.R. China
> **Tel:** 0086-10-1101056
> **E-mail:** bettyhello222@163.com

Case Study 3 is the reply from the Chinese company to the first enquiry from the American company.

Case Study 4: Checking about Models

> **To:** Jason Carter@abc.com
> **From:** Elena Williams@abc.com
> **Subject:** Checking about Models

> Dear Jason,
> Got it, thanks.
>
>   Are they all models of AVX that your company is using currently? Can Models of DEDOES be sent to us today?
>
> All the best!
> Elena

As shown in Case Study 4, this is an E-mail message being sent to the business partner whom Elena is very familiar with. In this case, Elena may get the response in a few seconds and reply at once as if she was talking on the phone. This makes the E-mail message like short conversations. People usually compose this kind of E-mail message less formally.

More Examples
Example 1: Appointment

> **From:** lilijess543@tvb.com
> **To:** jamesb211@tvb.com
> **BCC:** linda6789@abc.com
> **Subject:** Appointment for the ABC President Between Dec 4th-7th, 2016
>
> Dear Mr. Bond,
>   As per our earlier conversation, I am writing to schedule an appointment for our company's President, Ms. Nuvalle who is coming from New York on December 3rd. Would any time be convenient between December 4th and December 7th?
>   I would appreciate you letting me know as soon as possible the exact date and time so that we could continue planning Ms. Nuvalle's visit.
>
> With best regards,
Lili Jessica
>
> Lili Jessica (Ms.)
> CEO
> ABC Inc.
> **Add:** 300 Milky St., Los Angeles, CA 90015, USA
> **Tel:** 001-310-8765432
> **Fax:** 001-310-8765432
> **E-mail:** lilijess543@tvb.com

Example 2: Company and Product Introduction

To: Sydney Pierce
From: Lester Lenore
Date: Oct. 12th, 2016
Subject: TeleMundo Connections

Dear Mr. Pierce,

 Thank you for your inquiry into our Internet services. Telemundo Connections is an Internet service provider with a proven track record in customer service and satisfaction.

 Our technology and infrastructure is cutting edge—you'll find no other company with higher speed connection than Telemundo. We have several bundle packages, including landline/high speed Internet/cable services. Packages start at $29.95/month. For more information about which package would best suit your needs, please contact me at 555-333-8888.

Looking forward to serving you!

Yours faithfully,
Lester Lenore

Lester Lenore
Market Manager
Telemundo Inc.
Add: 450 Pine Ave, Los Angeles, CA 90015, USA
Tel: 001-310-2345678
E-mail: Lenorestrong@abc.com

Example 3: Talent Wanted

To: all staff
From: Mary Brown, CEO
Date: July 12th, 2016
Subject: A Personnel Manager Wanted

Dear all,

 Our company is looking for a new personnel manager for the next financial year in Italy. Five years' working experience and strong leadership are required. Fluent Italian is preferable. If you are interested in it, please send your CV and reference documents when applying.

Best wishes!

Mary

Example 4: Notification of Changes in Schedule

To: Mike Jones
From: Bill Smith, Sales Manager
Date: July 15th, 2016
Subject: Changes in Schedule

Dear Mike,

 I'm terribly sorry to inform you about the schedule change. The interview between us from 13:00–15:00 tomorrow has to be postponed since the period is to be occupied by an urgent meeting to be running the whole afternoon. The interview will be postponed on Wednesday July 17th. Your quick reply will be highly appreciated.

Yours sincerely,
Bill
Sales Manager

Example 5: Submission of Final Quarterly Sales Report

To: Janelle Williams
From: Carmichael Smith
Date: July 5th, 2016
Subject: Final Quarterly Sales Report
Attachment: Final Quarterly Sales Report

Dear Janelle,

 Please find attached to this E-mail the final version of the quarterly sales report. You will find that our numbers this year have been consistently encouraging.

 Comparing to the data from the prior quarter, we grossed approximately $8 million more this quarter. Even more exciting is the increase from the last fiscal year to the current year. We are now with about 20% more in profit.

 The report contains more specifics, please let me know if you have questions.

Regards!

Carmichael

Exercises

I. Fill in the blanks.

1. The format of an E-mail includes elements such as heading, _____, _____, _____, and signature.
2. Business E-mail writing should follow the principles of 6 "C", completeness, _____, _____, _____, correctness and _____.
3. Here are some tips for writing a business E-mail.
1) Identify the person whom you want to _____.
2) Write a _____ and _____ subject line.
3) Keep the message _____, concise and _____.
4) Don't _____.
5) Don't assume _____.
6) _____ before you send.
7) Respond _____.

II. Match the reasons in Column A with the openings in Column B.

Column A	Column B
Inviting	I am wondering if you'd like to…
Apologizing	Thank you for…
Informing	I'm writing to apologize for not…
Requesting	I'm writing to ask if you could…
Thanking	I'm writing to complain about…
Complaining	This is just to let you know that…

III. Replace each bold part with one word, making it more concisely expressed.

1. The new staff have been at the company for two weeks. **The new staff** seem to have settled in well.
2. Jonathan suggested that we postpone the meeting for a week. I think **postponing the meeting for a week** would be a good idea.
3. There are three items for discussion on today's agenda. The most important **item for discussion** is recruitment.

Chapter 3 Business E-mail

4. I look forward to **meeting up with** you on Friday.
5. We've been having problems finding well-qualified staff. **These kinds of** problems will hopefully be addressed in next month's meeting.
6. We will **make a decision** about the candidates by 10th February.
7. **In the normal course of events**, we hold department meetings on the first Tuesday of each month.
8. **In view of the fact that** the meeting room has been double-booked, I suggest we reschedule the meeting for 3rd July.

IV. **Simplify the following E-mail by deleting unnecessary words and expressions and reorganizing, making it concisely and clearly expressed.**

> The interview is taking place in two months' time—on 21st September, actually. Anyway, I'm not worrying about it, not at this moment in time at least. They said it'll be in Coventry at a hotel called Leofric Hotel. It's in the city centre, by the way.

V. **Exercises on formal and informal E-mail expressions.**

Section A   Rewrite the following sentences using the indirect polite expressions in the brackets.
1. I want an inventory of your products. (Could you…)
2. Leave us your contact details before you leave. (Would you…)
3. I need a taxi to pick me up from the airport at 10:30 on Monday. (Can you…)
4. Postpone the meeting to Tuesday, will you? (Would you mind…)
5. I want a prompt shipment. (Would it be possible…)
6. Give me an early reply. (I would be grateful if…)
7. Can you let me have some more details of the discounts you offer? (I would appreciate it if…)

Section B   Replace the bold part in each sentence with a more formal expression.
Example: **I'm happy to confirm** that your order has been dispatched.
            I have pleasure in confirming….
1. This is to **let you know** that your order has been processed.
2. **Can** I place an order by phone?
3. **I'm really sorry for** the delay to your order.
4. **Thanks a lot** for your order.
5. **Can** you confirm your contact details, please?
6. I hope you find the service **OK**.
7. I **got** your order this morning.

8. Can you **get in touch with** Janet Ahap?

Section C   Arrange the order of the following E-mails from the most formal to the least formal.

E-mail 1

| **To:** makki.e.rajaja@hort. Com |
| **From:** LaurenMajor@PTU.co.uk |
| **Subject:** Your Latest Order |

Dear Makki,

    I just want to let you know that I have got your order today. I'm really sorry, but we've run out of the blue folders. Can you get in touch and let me know whether red ones would be OK instead?

Best wishes
Lauren

E-mail 2

| **To:** m_nathan@nyh.com |
| **From:** J.martin@hort.com |
| **Subject:** Stationery Order of 12nd August |

Dear Mr. Nathan,

    Thank you for your stationery order of 12nd August. I have pleasure in confirming that the goods have been dispatched to you today.

    If you require any further information, or would like to place another order, please do not hesitate to contact me.

Yours sincerely,
Jean Martin
Sales Assistant

VI. Arrange the following sentences into the correct sequence of an E-mail of confirming an order.

  a. Margaret Nelmes (Customer Services Manager)
  b. Thank you for placing an order with BFT Direct.
  c. Your order is now being processed.
  d. Subject: Order No. 556865
  e. Once we have received the goods from our suppliers, you will be contacted to arrange a convenient delivery date.

f. Dear Miss Beech,

g. Alternatively, call our customer services division on 08933 388888.

h. Yours sincerely,

i. Meanwhile, if you wish to contact us regarding your order, please E-mail us on: fbt_order@fbt.com.

VII. Writing.

Writing 1

Situation: You and your manager David Bruce have appointed to meet each other 3 o'clock Tuesday to discuss the progress of the project you are responsible for. Unfortunately, you will be unable to meet him for some reasons. Write an E-mail explaining the matter and suggest other time for meeting.

To:
From:
Date:
Subject:

Writing 2

Situation: Your colleague Alice Jones in your office has helped you finish the project. Write an E-mail of thanks to her.

To:
From:
Date:
Subject:

Chapter 4

Business Memo

> **Brainstorm**
>
> (1) When you have a meeting in your class, how will you note down the agreement of the meeting? How will you declare the result of the meeting to the whole class?
>
> (2) In your opinion, what is the meaning of a record of meeting in a company?

扫描二维码
浏览视频
"How to Write a Perfect Memo"

To encourage action and serve as its collective memory, companies rely on three forms of mail besides letters: memo, voice mail, and E-mail. Although electronic technology is blurring the distinctions among these forms and changing the very meaning of mail, memos meet many of purposes of letters in making and responding to requests and maintaining relationships.

Generally, letters are usually written to those outside your company, while memos are usually sent internally. Both should be brief, preferably no more than one page. But, among other topics, reports on research or field investigations, describe policies and procedures, and circulate the minutes of meetings.

As letters look like letters, memos look like memos, and that look helps you determine the content appropriate for a memo. Memos begin with a *header*, which usually includes four items, preprinted on a memo form, most commonly in the following order.

```
To
From
Date
Subject
```

● **To.** When you write a letter, you generally address one person. In a memo, you may write to one person, but you often address a group of people: all employees, all collaborators of a project, all people who attended a meeting; that is, you write to a set of individuals. In selecting that set, be sparing. You may be tempted to include many,

but the more people named on a distribution list, the less likely it is that any one of them will read the memo, because each may think the other is taking care of the issue.
- **From.** Identify yourself as the sender of the document. Add a title to your name if the context requires that the reader know your title as well as your name.
- **Date.** Make sure your memo is timely, sent at the right time to meet a current need. Memos are fleeting documents, responding to a particular issue, at a particular time. But they are also permanent in creating a record for future reference. So if you write when you are angry, or say something indiscreet or without proper consideration, that memo may establish a record which later embarrasses you.
- **Subject.** Make the specific purpose of your memo clear in the subject line. Here's a simple rule: one memo=one topic or action. Announcing that topic or action in the subject line helps the reader decide how (perhaps "if") and when to read the memo. In the stream of project documentation represented by memos, each category of information—for example, costs, components, personnels—may find a home in a different file. Moreover, each action may require a different approval. So covering several topics in one memo may make responding, acting, filing, and approving difficult.

Under the header, you need to hit the point by offering a paragraph or paragraphs, which is the message that the memo wants to convey.
- **Opening paragraph.** Following the header, provide the memo's main content. Use a brief opening paragraph to make clear what your subject line implies. Answer this question, "Why am I reading this memo from you now and what should I do about it?" Give the context of your memo by expanding:

①What action or understanding you seek from the reader.
②Why you selected the reader to receive this message.
③Why you—rather than someone else—wrote the memo.
④Why you are sending it today—rather than yesterday or tomorrow.

If the memo responds to a request, note that request to remind the reader and engage her or his attention. The subject line and opening paragraph go a long way toward achieving the memo's purpose, so they deserve special care.
- **Supporting paragraphs.** In a series of short, well labeled paragraphs and perhaps a visual or two, provide the supporting argument.
- **Closing paragraph.** Note any action or decision the reader should take.

Sample 1

MEMO
To: Co-workers
From: Mike
Date: June 25th, 2016
Subject: Customer Presentation

> The P&G marketing presentation you prepared this Monday to demonstrate our product line was wonderful!
>
> Your sincerity, enthusiasm, salesman skill and expert knowledge impressed Mr. Han and thus sealed the deal with him.
>
> Thank you for your outstanding work and endeavor in the job, the bonus check will be distributed next week.
>
> My sincere congratulation to all of you!

Let's have a look at a sample of memo, which fails to realize its purpose of writing.

Sample 2

> **To:** Programmers
> **From:** T. Gray
>
> Due to the poor response in filing off documents, the system is still working at a high capacity. Although it had been urged that filing off be done regularly, it appears that no one has followed the correct procedure. Therefore, the system is working harder, and there have been several reports of malfunctions.
>
> In view of this, Maria Jones has asked me to advise you that the system will be reinitialized on Wednesday, June 22nd. In other words, the system will be cleaned out. This will result in shutdown of about 2 hours.
>
> You must file off all your documents no later than Tuesday, June 21st. As the reinitialized process deletes anything left in the system's disc, we will assume that you do not need any documents remaining in the system on June 22nd.
>
> Thank you for your cooperation.

This memo looks more like a note, not a memo. In the first paragraph, the writer expressed his anger about "no one following the correct procedure" of filing the document which leads to the trouble. Therefore the reader don't learn what the memo is about (the reinitialization) until the second paragraph.

In the final paragraph, the writer expressed a type of thanking in advance, which is ridiculous since people haven't cooperated. Thanking them for something they haven't done won't make them do it!

Here is a better way of writing the memo.

Sample 3

> On Wednesday, June 22nd, the system will be shut down for two hours to be reinitialized. Therefore, you must file off your documents no later than June 21st. Files remaining on the systems after that day will be purged.
>
> This reinitialization is needed because the system has been working at a high capacity as a result people fail to file off regularly. Once again, here's the procedure for filing off documents:
>
> ...

A well-organized memo may contain many components. Let's look at another memo.

Sample 4

MEMORANDUM

To: lab supervisors
From: safety department
Date: 1st Oct, 2016
Re: WARNING

Before 23rd October, please hang a tag with your name and lab number on any bypass lines around check/surge valves in your lab's gas line.
(requested action simply stated)

After that date, mechanics will start removing the lines. The work requires that we shut off the gas to any lab which has such a line.
(consequences of noncompliance)

Because of the potential for explosion, we are no longer allowing such bypasses. See my memo dated 10th September for more details. Shop mechanic have already identified 15 violations, but we need your help in tagging any others.
(rationale)

If you identify your lines, we can schedule their removal to fit your needs and thus avoid any interruption in service. If you wait until we identify them, then we will not be able to notify you in advance of their removal.
(benefit of requested action)

A fine-toned memo tells people some important information and demands people for future actions. It should not only present facts, but also indicate further requirements. Compare with the following memo. You can see how ineffective a memo may be if you don't follow the format of a memo. In the following memo, the writer has tried to include a lot of information, but the reader may not get his points.

MEMORANDUM

Date: May 1st, 2016
To: all staff
From: R. J. Nettleson, Head
Re: safety

Even though I have attended some recent safety meetings, it has been a while since a safety communicator has been generated by me. Well, I am still very interested in the subject both on my own and because it is still a heavy-duty item in the viewpoint of the company.

> We are chugging along toward two million man-hours without a lost-time accident and, if we all keep ourselves alert to safe practice, we will make it. A lot of people are looking forward to that late this year. It is my hope that we can knock off that milestone and go after several million more man-hours without a lost-time accident in the future.
>
> The reality is, unfortunately, that someday someone will have a lost-time accident, and I want to address that eventuality today. The larger our number of man-hours gets, the worse the person who finally causes it to end will feel. That is why, before we know who that will be, I am writing that follows. Both myself and the unlucky sole will feel extremely bad when it happens. Please don't chide or ride or make light of the fact that they were responsible. I feel that the vast majority of people and maybe all would not do that and do not need the request.
>
> Additionally, as a continued enhancement of our safety efforts, we will be conducting an international safety rating system baseline audit of R&D sometime in July. It is designed to show us where we are weak so we can improve. This will be coordinated by John Jones who will communicate additional information further down the road.
>
> Thank you for your time and have a good and safe summer.

A memo serves not only a document to convey information, but also a document for record. Sometimes, people use memo as a minute. Then, the memo should:

① Begin with the meeting's agenda and summarize the results on each point.

② Note any conclusions arrived at in the meeting.

③ List assignments (actions to be taken) with the names of those responsible for performing them.

④ Confirm any deadlines.

⑤ Streamline the record of the discussion.

⑥ Note any subsequent meetings.

⑦ Attach any documents circulated during the meeting as an appendix.

⑧ Ask the reader to validate the correctness of the record.

Sample 5

> **MEMORANDUM**
>
> **Date:** April 14th, 2016
> **To:** Marketing group
> **From:** Paula Petersen
> **Re:** Minutes of 12nd April Meeting on Web Marketing
>
> **Attending:** Steve, Amy, Kasha, Paula (Quinn was on assignment)
> *(attendees for the record)*

> The MG met to determine if, and how, we should market on the web. Steve reported on a recent conference he attended about technical marketing on the Internet (see attached report). He strongly recommended that we develop a web page for our photochemical and extend the approach to other products if the response warrants.
> *(purpose and overview)*
>
> **Discussion centered on three issues:**
> 1. *Cost.* In general, except for the onetime costs of start-up and development, the cost of such marketing is much lower than though traditional media.
> 2. *Effectiveness.* At this point, it's hard to determine how effective such marketing is. We discussed this at some length.
> 3. *Ease of operation.* Steve assured us the learning curve is not all that steep: we should be able to develop and run the web site by ourselves without additional hiring or extensive work.
>
> *(list form eases skimming)*
>
> **Action**
> > *Steve.* Develop a prototype web page for photochemical.
> >
> > *Amy.* Survey local web access providers to check on fees, requirements, etc.
> >
> > *Kasha.* Review our competitors' web pages (if there are any) and in general browse the web for ideas.
> >
> > *Quinn.* Outline a document package that would include the information for the web page and supporting follow-up documents.
>
> *(clearly defines each attendee's further responsibilities)*
>
> **Next meeting:** 1st, May, 3 P. M. in the conference room
> **Agenda:** reports on the actions listed above
> *(uses highlighting to remind readers about the net meeting)*

There are too many kinds of memos written in the life of a business writer. The following tips on writing memos can be applied widely.

1. Use a Person's Name and Title Whenever Possible

People like their names used and spelled correctly. Usually, a phone call to the person's office or organization will give you that information. If you can't get the person's name, then use a generic title to address your reader.

For example, if you're writing to a department store for credit, write to *"Dear Credit Manager"*. Avoid vague salutations in letters such as *"To Who it May Concern"* or *"Dear Sir/Madam"*. If you send your letter to someone specific, the letter is more likely to be taken seriously and not passed around from person to person than if you address the memo vaguely.

If you address a wide variety of people, use a generic title such as *"Dear Reader" "Dear Technical-service Managers"* and the like.

If you know the name but not the sex of the reader, we suggest you use the full name in the salutation without identifying the sex, for example, *"Dear Terry Smith"* or *"Dear Leslie Fahrenkrug"*.

2. Use a Re Line to Signal the Subject Matter of the Memo

Re line is an optional separate line above the salutation and below the reader's address. Re lines can be useful in memos to highlight key details for quick reference, such as relevant invoice numbers, dates of past conversations or correspondences, file numbers, or client names.

Re lines also orient the reader as to the content and nature of the communicator.
For example:

"Re: Your Upcoming Performance Review of 1/4/16"

It's especially helpful to remind readers that you are writing about a topic on which you've had a previous communicator.
For example:

"Re: September reorganization of ORACLE database"

Or you are responding to some others.
For example:

"Re: Your Memo of 9/2/16"

Re lines hold information you might otherwise be forced to place in the opening sentences of your memo. If you use Re line, you can avoid such awkward opening sentences as *"In response to your August 2nd letter regarding Ed and Martha Colby's account…"*, just put the date of the letter, the names, and the account number in the Re line:

Re: Response to August 2nd Letter about Ed and Martha Colby's Account

Then start, *"After researching the missing interest in the Colby's account, I found…"*

In memos, the Re line is usually placed two lines directly beneath the date. Here are three examples of succinct re lines:

Re: Need to Improve Product Movement
Re: Weekly Progress—August 16th, 2016
Re: Expectorant PH Values of Tartar-control Pastes

3. Give Your Reason for Writing in the First Paragraph

As in all other forms of writing, memo writing requires you to be organized. If you put too many details in the first paragraph or fail to get to the point of your message, your reader may not stay with the memo long enough to find the important information.

Certainly, there are exceptions to this rule. You might not do it in a memo to a subordinate. Nor would you do it when you want to use your first paragraph to thank someone for doing something or to bridge a gap from an earlier communication. The important issue is to avoid meandering into your idea so that you fail to get to the point, or get it three or four paragraphs into the message.

4. Establish an Appropriate Order for Your Responses

If your memo is in response to an earlier communication, you should answer any questions that were asked—but not necessarily in the same order. Although generally it's a good idea to answer questions in the order they're brought up, recognize that some writers ask questions in no particular sequence other than the order in which they occur to the writer. In these situations, you must take control by organizing your responses according to your own logic. And if you can anticipate the kind of information your reader will need, you'll spare both your reader and yourself the need for additional correspondence.

5. Keep the Memo Brief

People neither expect nor want long memos. If possible, limit memo to one or two pages. The same goes for sentences and paragraphs. Keep them short and to the point. We recommend limiting the first paragraph to one or two sentences, subsequent paragraphs can be longer.

If you have a lot to say, you can extend your memo to two pages. You have other options too. Enclose a separate report containing the statistical or factual details, saving your memo for the highlights of the message. Too often, people refuse to read memos that are more than a page long—they lose interest.

6. End Your Memo by Telling the Reader What Happens Next

Whether you need a response by a certain date, want someone's approval on something, or just want the recipient to know what you'll do next, let your reader know in the closing sentence. For example, *"Please sign the form and send it to me by January 6th"* and *"I'll give you a call on Tuesday to follow up"* are specific closing sentences.

These sentences avoid the vague statements, such as *"Thanking you in advance"* (Don't thank people for doing something they haven't done—or agreed to do) or *"If you have any questions, please feel free to contact me"*.

It's all right to end on a vague note occasionally, since we don't always have specific actions and firm commitments upon which to comment. When just keeping in touch or being cordial, there's nothing wrong with an ending with *"I look forward to seeing you soon"*. But don't use a close like *"If you have any questions…"* when the memo you've written is so straightforward and simple that one would probably not have questions.

7. Be Professional in Writing

You need to identify with the case or situation when writing a memo. Write in the first person (we or I) to the client or recipient (you). They or other third person is rarely used. Be empathetic to where the recipient may be coming from. The problems you uncover may have started with the addressee!

Be concise and fact based. Long winded and circuitous writing will lose your audience—often the person who pays your salary (boss or client)—this is not good. One page is your goal with data or background attached as additional pages.

Write for impact. Think of a memo more like a resume—use subtitles, bullets, underpinning, highlighting/ bolding, numbering, in order to make your key points.

Avoid loaded words. Words that are strong in an academic, or informal context, can be highly problematic in business. Samples include: *dominate, destroy, discriminate*—all can end up being used against your company in court for issues such as anti-trust proceedings or lawsuits.

Use proper language /grammar. There is a reason you have your thesaurus and dictionary. False familiarity can also be a major faux pas.

Recommend actions to resolve issues and problems. Be specific and practical.

Be clear on next steps to have action taken—keep the ball rolling. "I will call you Monday" type messages show urgency and a willingness to lead.

Finally, remember that memos are NOT E-mails. While they may be sent electronically, they are purposeful and professional, not careless nor causal in language or tone. All correspondences in a company are subject to subpoena and retrieval, so never send anything in anger, nor haste. Many memos are written in draft and may take 3 edits to complete over hours to a day.

Exercises

I. Fill in the blanks.

1. Generally, letters are usually written to those _____ your company, while memos are usually sent _____.
2. The common elements of a memo include to, _____, date, _____, opening paragraph, supporting paragraph and closing paragraph.
3. A fine-toned memo tells people some important _____ and demands people for future _____.

4. Re lines can be useful in both letters and memos to highlight _____ for quick reference, such as relevant invoice numbers, dates of past conversations or correspondences, file numbers, or client names.

5. People neither expect nor want long memos. If possible, limit memo to _____ or _____ pages. The same goes for sentences and paragraphs. Keep them _____ and _____.

II. **Writing.**

Your company is planning to enter into the market of the Repulic of Korea. The Board of Director decided to hold a meeting with all managers in different departments. In the meeting, people will discuss and brainstorm about the promotion campaign and the launching of a new product. The company will agree to publish advertisement in some media of the Republic of Korea. Please write a memo to inform all managers to attend the meeting.

Chapter 5

Business Report

> **Brainstorm**
>
> (1) Have you ever tried writing a report? If yes, what subject was your report about?
> (2) In your opinion, what are the difficult points in writing a report in English?

扫描二维码
浏览视频
"Effective
Business Report
Writing"

A report furnishes a permanent record of some work and its outcome. It is the document in which engineers, scientists, and managers transmit the results of their research, field work, and other activities to people in their organization. Here's what the University of Rochester's Department of Chemical Engineering has to say about engineers and report writing:

"The importance of being able to write a good report cannot be emphasized too strongly. The chemical engineer who carries out an investigation or study has not completed his job until he has submitted a report on the project. The true value of the project and the abilities of the investigator may be distorted or unrecognized unless the engineer is able to write a commendable report."

Reports also help individuals and organizations find more efficient methods of production, raise profits, develop new products or markets, and meet social and environmental responsibilities. Often, a written report is the only tangible product of hundreds of hours of works. Rightly or wrongly, the quality and worth of that work are judged by the quality of the written report—its clarity, organization, and content. Therefore, it pays to take the time to write a good report. People produce a number of different types of reports, summarized in Table 5-1.

Table 5-1 Types of Reports

Type	Description and purpose
Periodic report	Report submitted at regular intervals to provide information on the activities or status of the organization. Bank statements, annual reports, and call reports are examples of periodic reports.

Continued

Type	Description and purpose
Progress report	Update on an ongoing activity as it is being carried out. The activity may be construction, expansion, research and development, production, or other projects.
Research report	Results of research, studies, and experiments conducted in the lab or in the field.
Field report	Results of an on-site inspection or evaluation of some field activity, which might be construction, pilot-plant tests, or equipment installation and setup.
Recommendation report	Report submitted to management as the basis for decisions or actions. It makes recommendations on such subjects as whether to fund a research program, launch a project, develop a new product, buy a piece of capital equipment, or acquire a company or technology.
Feasibility report	Report that explores the feasibility of undertaking a particular project, venture, or commitment. It examines and compares alternatives, analyzes the pros and cons, and suggests which, if any, of the alternatives are feasible.

When composing a report, first determine your purpose in writing the report. That purpose also reflects the reader's reason for reading the report. Two major purposes for writing are to inform and to persuade; similarly, two major purposes for reading are to understand and to decide or act. Although informing and persuading can overlap, it's helpful to think of one major purpose as you select and structure information.

As the purposes of reports differ, they are structured in different formats. Therefore, the information needed might differ drastically. Then the writer needs to utilize his understanding of the purpose to focus on his choice. Let's have a look at the structures of two reports.

Sample 1: Progress Report

A. **Heading:** identify project, purpose, time period
B. **Introduction:** previous work completed
C. **Present status**
 1. Present work
   a. Work completed
   b. Work started
 2. Problems
D. Work remaining
 1. Work planned next
 2. Assessment of progress
   a. To date
   b. To completion

Sample 2: A Feasibility Report

> 1 Introduction
> 2 Research findings
> 3 Analysis of research findings
>   3.1 Pros
>   3.2 Cons
> 4 Conclusion of facts and analyses
> 5 Recommendations

Lastly design the information to achieve your purpose. Various formats serve different types of reports and the selected information showcases and highlights the purposes of them.

All reports need to be clear, concise and well structured. The key to writing an effective report is to allocate time for planning and preparation. With careful planning, the writing of a report will be made much easier. The essential stages of successful report writing are described below.

Stage One: Understanding the report brief

You need to understand the purpose of the report as described in your report brief or instructions. Consider who the report is for and why it is being written. Check the time before the deadline between the different stages. Be sure to leave time for final proof reading and checking.

Stage Two: Gathering and selecting information

You need to gather any relevant information. The information may come from a variety of sources, but how much information you will need will depend on how much detail is required in the report. You may want to begin by reading relevant literature to widen your understanding of the topic or issue before you go on to look at other forms of information such as questionnaires, surveys, etc. As you read and gather information, you need to assess its relevance to your report and select accordingly. Keep referring to your report brief to help you decide what relevant information is.

Stage Three: Organizing material

After you have gathered information you need to decide what will be included and in what sequence it should be presented. Begin by grouping together points that are related. These may form sections or chapters. Choose an order for your material that is logical and easy to follow.

Stage Four: Analyzing the material

Before you begin to write your first draft of the report, take time to consider and make notes on the points you will make, using the facts and evidence you have gathered. What conclusions can be drawn from the material? What are the limitations or flaws in the evidence? It is not enough to simply present the information you have gathered. You must relate it to the problem or issue described in the report brief.

Stage Five: Writing the report

When you begin to write the report, you may find it easier to write the summary and contents page at the end since you know exactly what will be included. Avoid waffle and make your points clearly and concisely. Chapters, sections and even individual paragraphs should be written with a clear structure. The structure described below can be adapted and applied to chapters, sections and even paragraphs.

- Introduce the main idea of the chapter/ section/paragraph.
- Explain and expand the idea, defining any key terms.
- Present relevant evidence to support your points.
- Comment on each piece of evidence showing how it relates to your points.
- Conclude your chapter/section/paragraph by either showing its significance to the report as a whole or making a link to the next chapter/section/paragraph.

Stage Six: Reviewing and redrafting

Ideally, you should leave time to take a break before you review your first draft. Be prepared to rearrange or rewrite sections in the light of your review. Try to read the draft from the perspective of the reader. Is it easy to follow with a clear structure that makes sense? Are the points concisely but clearly explained and supported by relevant evidence? Writing on a word processor makes it easier to rewrite and rearrange sections of paragraphs in your first draft. If you write your first draft by hand, try writing each section on a separate piece of paper to make redrafting easier.

Stage Seven: Presentation

Once you are satisfied with the content and structure of your redrafted report, you can turn your attention to the presentation. Check that the wording of each chapter/section/subheading is clear and accurate. Check that you have adhered to the instructions in your report brief regarding formal presentation. Check for consistency in numbering of chapters, sections and appendices. Make sure that all your sources are acknowledged and correctly referenced. You will need to proofread your report for errors of spelling or grammar. If time allows, proofread more than once. Errors in presentation or expression create a poor impression and can make the report difficult to read.

Recommendation: Evaluating your report

Evaluation of a report you have written can give benefits. In a group project, it is not good enough to have one person write the report and another person read it. You need to read by yourself or by someone else the report critically and methodically. You need to see if each of the aspects mentioned above in the structure of the report is covered. It may even help to have a check-list, although with experience this becomes unnecessary.

- Check if the title/abstract makes sense.
- Are all the relevant questions answered in the introduction?

- Is the overall structure of the rest of the sections meaningful?
- Is there difference from related/past work?
- Are the technical sections understandable? Are the figures/tables explained properly? Is the terminology clear? Are the symbols used defined appropriately?
- Are the results explained properly? Are the conclusions drawn from the graphs/tables sound? Or are there technical holes/flows? Do the results show how the work presented is better/worse than the other cases of comparison?

Although reports can take many forms, most contain the following major sections: front matter, introduction, body, ending and back matter. Let's go to each section precisely.

1. Front Matter

Front matter includes cover and title page, abstract, table of contents and list of illustrations.

- *Cover and Title Page.* The cover and the title page create the reader's first impression of the report. The cover should be cleanly typed but not gaudy; do not try to fancy it up with borders, stars, or similar treatments. The title page should give the tile, the report number, the author's name, the organization for which the report was produced, and the date on which the report is submitted. Other information can be added as necessary.

- *Abstract.* The abstract (or summary) is an informative, concise, one-paragraph statement of the work performed, its objectives and scope, and the major conclusions reached. There are two types of abstract: one is informative abstract—a tightly condensed version of the actual information contained in the body of the report. Another is the descriptive abstract—a description of what the body of the reports covers.

Abstract, or executive summary (popular in business writings for corporate or government reports) is highly valuable for readers, who are more likely to read that than any other part of a report or article. All the audiences of a document with an abstract will at least skim the abstract:

- Managers who might not read the technical discussion in a report.
- Accountants interested in a general overview of a project.
- Cataloging librarians who just need to know where to file a document.
- Researcher perusing a collection of abstracts to determine if they should consult a parent document; sometimes the abstract contains all the information the researcher needs.
- Attendees at conferences reviewing abstracts in a preliminary program to decide which events to attend and to formulate the questions they wish to ask of the speakers.
- Program chairs of conferences to determine which proposed papers to accept for presentation.

A descriptive abstract (sometimes called a topical abstract) briefly indicates the topics covered in the parent document. It provides no conclusions or supporting evidence and rarely exceeds one or two sentences regardless of the length of the original.

> *This article discusses a Singapore-based research project that analyzed how cultural background affects an applicant's performance in a job interview.*

Informative abstract tells more for readers who need more information. It doesn't talk about the report or article but about the investigation. It provides the content of a document in a nutshell.

> *In a country like Singapore, which is rated high in power distance and low in individualism (using Hofstede's dimensions of national cultures), interviews for entry-level positions in multinational corporations (MNCs) may reveal subtle clashes in culture. To test this hypothesis, we analyzed transcripts of job interviews involving nine English-speaking applicants from Chinese backgrounds and two experienced interviewers form Anglo-American MNCs in Singapore. Our assumption was that a person's cultural background and upbringing influence his or her performance at job interview. The findings reveal that Chinese applicants tend to defer to the interviewer and focus on the group or family, besides being averse to self-assertion. Hence, applicants from a Chinese background may be disadvantaged when being interviewed for jobs with MNCs which are heavily influenced by Anglo-American culture.*

In practice, the neat distinction between informative and descriptive abstracts is sometimes blurred. Therefore, a hybrid abstract is often pursued.

> *Despite the increasing interdependence of global economies, there is surprisingly little cooperative product development done by related international divisions of multinational industrial corporations. Cooperative development could offer multinational corporations the means to pool expertise and other resources available in various regions to produce globally competitive products. The two main obstacles are the failure of management to recognize the extent to which sociocultural aspects affect their own decision-making processes and those of their international counterparts; and even having recognized that sociocultural aspects have a significant impact, more managers are ill prepared to deal with them. A case study is presented of a large Swiss electronic-equipment manufacturer with a US subsidiary in the same field. Qualitative and descriptive data from interviews with managers and engineers are reported and related to the sociocultural backdrop in which they make their decisions. Recommendations and areas of further study are also presented.*

- **Table of Contents.** The table of contents lists every section heading and subheading and the page number on which they appear, except itself, the title page, and the abstract. Tables, figures, charts, and graphs are listed separately at the end.

- *List of Illustrations*. If more than four illustrations are used in the body of the report, the number and the title of each should be listed along the corresponding page number. Both figures and tables should be included as illustrations.

2. Introduction

The introduction introduces the reader to the body of the report. It tells the reader the following: ①What the report is about. ②Why the report was written. ③How the body is developed. The introduction tells readers—including those not familiar with the subject matter or the reason for writing the report—the purpose of the report. It also provides background material, theory, and explanation of why the work was done and what it accomplished.

- Present the nature and the scope of the investigated problem.
- Put into perspective the importance of the research as it relates to scientific knowledge or commercial operations.
- Discuss findings from previous research and other pertinent literature, if such material exists.
- State the methods of investigation.
- Present the key results of the research.

Here's an example of an introduction of a technical report.

> *Marketing had requested R&D to research conditions under which E-Z Bond dentifrice formulations could prove harmful. In response, R&D conducted acute oral toxicity tests on the current dentifrice formulation, which contains 0.8% NaMFP, and two experimental dentifrice formulations containing 1.6% and 2.4% NaMFP, respectively.*
>
> *Each of the dentifrice formulations was administered by oral intubation into male rat at dosage of 30 grams per kg of body weight, then to three groups of female rats at dosages of 30, 15 and 10 grams per kg of body weight.*
>
> *Subjects were evaluated for appearance and behavior, weight loss, mortality, and gross pathology at necropsy. No mortality was observed in any of the tests.*

3. Body

The body is the largest and most important section of the report. All the other components are meant to support and lend credibility to this section. Usually, the body should contain at least the methods, the results, and the conclusions or findings of research. Sometimes, it also includes *overview of literature, observation of status quo, analysis of strong and weak points of subject matter, opportunities and threats, problems and solutions,* etc.

4. Ending

A report should be ended skillfully to fulfil its purpose. The ending may include a *summary*, *conclusions* and *recommendations*.

The summary presents the results of the report, along with the discussion of the meaning, significance, and application of the results.

The conclusions are a series of numbered statements showing how the results answered questions raised in the stated purpose of the research. On the basis of results and conclusions, the writer can make recommendations, i.e. whether further actions are needed or how the results can be applied commercially. A reader can often predict your recommendations based on your conclusions, but they are not the same. Conclusions look to the past; recommendations look to the future. Here is one segment from the recommendation section of a report on *"Growth in a Global Environment"*.

> *The Global Climate Coalition recommends a policy including the following opinions:*
> - *Accelerate the pace of research into basic climate science and impact assessment.*
> - *Identify and pursue measures that will reduce the threat of climate change, yet also make sense in their own right.*
> - *Establish sustained research and development programs that improve the ability to economically produce and utilize energy with less potential for the accumulation of greenhouse gases.*
> - *Expand efforts to understand and communicate the economic, social, and political consequences of both climate change and proposed policy responses.*

5. Back Matter

The back matter offers supporting materials necessary to the report. It might include the *references, appendixes,* etc.

The references include an alphabetical bibliography, the symbols used in the report and the proper unit of measure for each.

While the appendixes contain any sample calculations, tables, diagrams or graphs, mathematical derivations, sets of measurements, calibration data, or computer printouts that are too long, cumbersome, or unimportant to be included in the main body of the report.

A report is a document that defines a subject or problem, and gathers relevant information and facts in order to present them as completely and accurately as possible. A report may include analysis, judgment, conclusions and recommendations. So a report therefore needs to be:

- Brief.

- Understandable.
- Precise.
- Logically structured.
- Descriptive.
- Aimed at the reader.

In terms of the language in writing the report, you need to pay attention to the following points:

- Make sure you mention the background to, and aims of the investigation.
- Include the basic concepts and theory relating to the investigation.
- Describe the procedures used. Identify major sources of error and explain who they were dealt with.
- Only data directly relevant to the calculation of final results should be presented, omit raw data. Graphs are a particularly effective way of presenting results—only use table where it would make more sense than providing a graph.
- Final results should be presented clearly and concisely. Include an analysis of errors, but omit details of arithmetical manipulations.
- If a computer code was used or written, give details of the checks and validations you performed on the code.
- The interpretation of the results must be discussed, and improvements and possible extensions of the work suggested.
- Give references to any books, articles or other sources of information that have proved useful in preparing the report, or carrying out the work.

You may have spent days, weeks, or months gathering information and writing a lengthy report. If the report doesn't have visual appeal, however, nobody will read it or understand it. Visuals provide a subtle unconscious signal that the document is worth readers' attention. When a document has visual impact, it attracts attention, invites readership, and establishes the credibility of your message even before you state your case.

- **Visual impact organizes information.** A good visual design breaks the document into manageable, bite-sized chunks, making it easy for readers to find the key pieces of information. The readers can concentrate on one idea at a time.
- **Visual impact emphasizes what's important.** You can create a hierarch of information so that your readers can separate major points from supporting ones—much like you see in newspapers. In today's hurried world where people are pulling their hair out because of tight schedules, your readers will appreciate a quick read.

1. Using White Space

White space is a key ingredient in visual design. It includes all areas on the page or where there's neither type nor graphics. White space doesn't have to be white. For example, if your paper or screen background is ivory, tan or whatever, the background color is called white space. White space can make the report inviting and approachable, provide contrast and a resting place for the readers' eyes, and create the impression that the document is easy to read.

> **Tips for White Space**
> - For paper documents, use 1 to 1.5 inch top, bottom, and side margins to create a visual frame around all the text and graphic.
> - Double-space between paragraphs to help the reader see each paragraph as a separate unit.
> - Emphasize key pieces of text (words, phrases, or paragraphs) with white space or a different font.

2. Give Me a Break

It's crucial to break your sentences and paragraphs into manageable, bite-sized chunks of information. Many report writers use long sentences and dense paragraphs. Doing so makes information difficult to digest and causes readers to tune out. When you optimize sentence and paragraph length, you give your documents more visual appeal. One way to stick to the 25-word limit is to look for compound sentences—you know, those separated by *and, but,* or other conjunctions. And limit paragraphs to 8 lines.

Think of your paragraphs as trains of thought. When one train leaves the station, another train arrives that heads in the same general direction. Although there are no hard and fast rules about paragraph length, when you limit each paragraph to 8 lines, you have a very readable document.

3. Harness the Visual Power of Headlines

Newspapers and magazines use informative headlines as guideposts for visual impact. The headlines tell a story and direct the readers to what's important. When you write compelling headlines, readers skim the message. As a reader you get the gist of the text and find key information quickly.

> **Informative:**
> Quarterly Inspections Cut Accident Rates By 23%
> **Non-informative:**
> Report of Quarterly Inspections
>
> **Informative:**
> Conclusion: We Need to Conduct Further Tests
> **Non-informative:**
> Conclusion

> **Informative:**
> Findings: There Is No Critical Difference Between the Control Group and the Experimental Group
> **Non-informative:**
> Findings

4. Put It on the List

A list can help streamline information. Use bulleted lists when rank and sequence aren't important. Bullets give everything on the list equal value. Always head the list with a descriptive sentence, as you see in the following example.

> **Following is my shopping list:**
> - Two bottles of mineral water
> - 1 kg of wheat flour
> - 3 kg of rice

Or you may use numbered list. It can show items in order of priority. Doing so gives the reader a visual clue that the items on the list are in priority order.

> Please take care of these issues first thing in the morning. Thanks.
> 1) Call the ABC Agency to arrange for a consultant for the week of March 15.
> 2) Ask Jim to prepare his R&D report.
> 3) Schedule a meeting with everyone involved in the project for the week I return.

Numbered list can also describe steps in a procedure, as well quantify items. Thus you can save your brain for more important things. Please punctuate properly, use parallel structures, and break lists into manageable chunks of information.

Whether you use a bullet or numbered list, create items that are parallel in structure. That means all elements that function alike must be treated alike. For example, in the parallel bulleted list that follows, all the bulleted items are gerunds—they end with *ing*. In the nonparallel bulleted list, the first two items end with *ing*, making the last item stick out like a wart at the end of your nose.

When making list, you also need to avoid laundry lists. When you have too many items on a list, you create a laundry list and readers may just gloss over everything you worked so hard to emphasize. Instead of creating a long list of bulleted or numbered items, break the items into categories. In the following example, you will see how dividing the list into two logical chunks of information is easier to read and gives more information.

Laundry list

> **Our global expansion takes us into the following countries:**
> - China
> - Indonesia
> - Malaysia
> - Portugal
> - Spain
> - Sweden
> - Thailand

Logical chunks of bulleted information

> **Our global expansion takes us into the following countries:**
>
> Asia
> - China
> - Indonesia
> - Malaysia
> - Thailand
>
> Europe
> - Portugal
> - Spain
> - Sweden

5. Use the Sequence That Works Best

As a writer, you must decide which sequence will have the impact you want to have on your readers. Table 5-2 shows a variety of methods for specific information flows.

Table 5-2 Methods for Specific Information Flows

Information flow	Method	Uses
Cause and effect	Show a plausible relationship between a situation and its causes or effects.	Experiments, accident reports
Chronological	Arrange events in sequential order to stress the relationship of what happened and when. Begin with the first event and continue to the last.	Trip reports, trouble reports, minutes of meetings, work schedule, manufacturing or scientific procedures, test protocols

Continued

Information flow	Method	Uses
Comparison	Point out similarities or differences, or advantages and disadvantage. (Tables or graphs are great ways to present these.)	Feasibility studies, research results, trends and forecasts
Decreasing order of importance	Start with the most important point and end with the least important point.	Reports for decision makers who make decisions based on the most important point
Division and classification	Divide complex topics into small chunks of information.	Processes, instructions
General and classification	Begin with a general statement and then provide facts to support it.	Reports, memos
Increasing order of importance	Start with the least important point and end with the most important point.	Personnel goals, oral presentations
Sequential	Explain something step by step.	Instructions, user manuals
Spatial	Describe an item according to the grouping of its physical features. This relates to where things are from east to west, north to south, left to right, top to bottom, interior or exterior.	Activity reports, layout of equipment, building sites, research reports
Specific to general	Start with a specific statement and build to a conclusion. A good tool for persuasive writing.	Analogies, work orders, customer service responses, feasibility reports

6. Picture

Charts and graphs are super ways to make your point very effectively. You can gather data and prepare a chart to display your findings, identify opportunities as a result of what visual appears, and update the data to show changes or progress.

Keep these tips in mind when you prepare charts and graphs:

• **Write a descriptive title.** Place the title above the chart or graph.

• **Use an appropriate scale.** For example, if your financial range is from $100 to $200, don't show a scale of $100 to $500.

• **Create a legend if the chart isn't self-explanatory.** Legends explain the symbols that appear in the chart.

- **Keep the design simple.** Eliminate any information your readers don't need to know.
- **Prepare a separate chart of graph for each point.** If you try to squeeze too much information on one graph, you defeat your purpose of making it simple to read.

If a picture is truly worth a thousand words, you can eliminate the thousand words with a well-done graphic. Make the graphic self-contained, tie it to the text, and place it as close to the text as possible. Clearly label all the charts as the graphic is self-explanatory and sends a clear message.

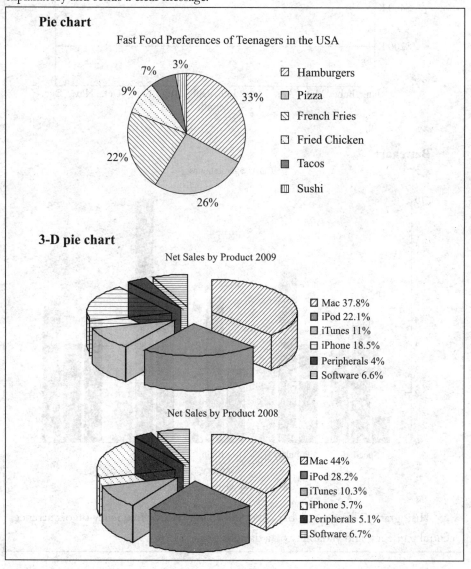

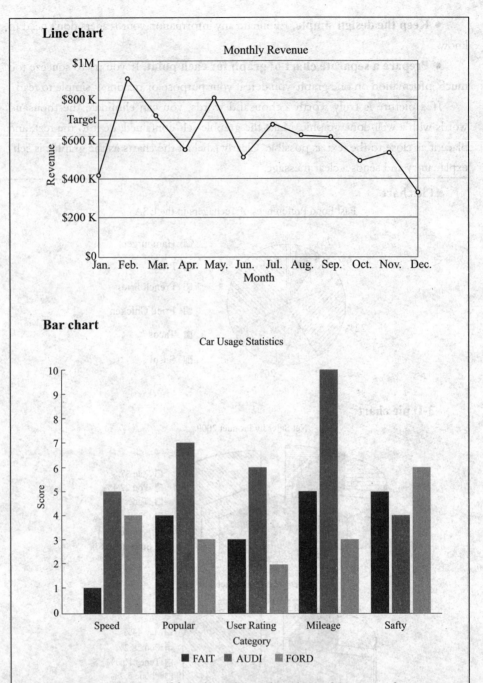

Histogram (This type of bar chart shows the relative frequency of occurrence, central tendency, and variability of a data set.)

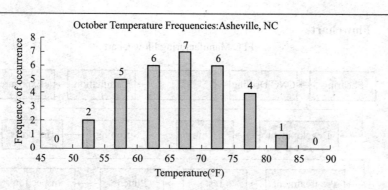

Pareto chart (This type of bar chart separates vital information from the trivial information.)

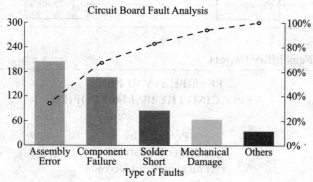

Scatter chart (This type of bar chart displays a relationship between two variables. It helps pinpoint the cause of a problem or shows how one variable may relate to another.)

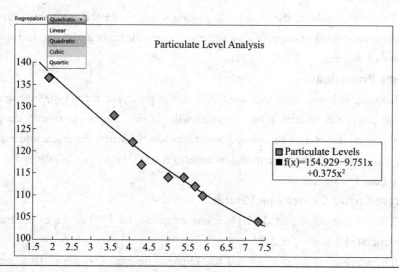

Flowchart

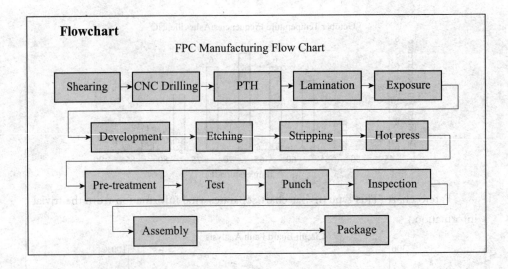

A Sample of Feasibility Report

**FEASIBILITY REPORT
REPLACING THE IBM 1403 COPIER**

**Prepared by
Roger Bernstein
Technical Services Division**

The purpose of this study is to determine whether Bateson Manufacturing Company should replace its high-volume copier to meet projected increases in printing volumes.

This study looks at the projected copying volumes for the company, alternate copiers as compared to the present equipment, operator times and costs, and special features of copiers.

Volume Projections

Copying volumes have increased 29% in the past year, from 140,000 pages to 180,000 pages per month. New contracts will increase pages-per-month demand to 200,000 by the end of this year. Projections based on new contracts and market surveys indicate a growth in copying volume to 300,000 pages per month by the end of the next 3 years.

Current Copier Capacity and Status

The present copier, an IBM 1403, has a capacity of 150,000 pages per month when operated 8 hours per day.

The machine is 3 years old and has required no major repairs in that time. A maintenance fee that covers all repair costs is paid monthly. Estimated machine life is 6 years. Surveys of other users have supported this estimate:

1. Grosbck Inc. —This company has operated the IBM 1403 on a full-time basis for the past 4 years with no major repairs.

2. Quay International —This company recently replaced their IBM 1403 after 6 years of full-time service with one major repair.

3. Quinby and Associates—The IBM 1403 at this company has been operated full time for 4.5 years with no major repairs needed.

Running the IBM 1403 on an overtime basis would proportionally lower the estimated machine life. Running 200,000 pages per month would add overtime usage that would decrease the approximately 3 years of remaining machine life to 2.5 years.

Furthermore, the IBM 1403 copier has been continued and cannot be replaced with the same model.

Operator Overtime

Operator salary rates are currently $7.39 per hour, with overtime paid at time and a half, or $11.09 per hour. Operator currently works about 2 hours of overtime a day to meet the copying demand of 180,000 pages per month. Overtime will increase to more than 2.5 hours a day by the end of the year, when the new contracts increase volume to 200,000 pages per month.

Other Copiers

Two alternate copiers were investigated as replacements for the IBM 1403. They are the IBM 3211 and the Xerox 8700. These machines represent improvements in duplicator technology within the medium price range. They were selected by the Batson Purchasing Department after industry surveys.

Both of the alternative copiers are capable of 200,000 pages per month without operator overtime. A comparison of the monthly basic operating costs of all three machines is presented in Table 1.

Table 1   Monthly Operating Costs at 200,000 Pages per Month

ITEM	IBM 1403($)	IBM 3211($)	Xerox 8700($)
Lease cost	568	1,108	3,733
Paper cost	1,820	2,080	550
Meter charge	None	None	2,100
Maintenance	1,187	1,269	0*
Tape drive	418	344	0**
Operator salary	1,721	1,686	1,084
Operator overtime	860	—	—
Sales tax	39	0*	0*
Totals	6,613	6,467	6,972

*Included in lease cost

**Not required at this volume

Paper Costs

The two IBM copiers use pin-fed, fan-fold computer paper at a cost of $9.10 per thousand sheets for the IBM 1403 and $10.30 per thousand sheets for the IBM 3211. The Xerox copier can also print on both sides of the paper; the IBM copiers cannot. Ninety percent of the company's duplicating can be done using both sides of the paper, reducing paper usage to 550 sheets on the Xerox for every one thousand sheets on the IBM copiers. This ratio is reflected in the paper costs in Table 1.

Paper costs have risen 18% over the summer and are predicted to rise by 25% by year's end. With a 25% increase in paper costs inserted into Table 1, the new monthly operation costs would be as follows:

IBM 1403	IBM 3211	Xerox 8700
$7,068	$6,982	$7,110

Indications are that paper costs will continue to rise. Another increase of 25%, which could occur as early as the first quarter of next year, would make the monthly cost of operating either IBM copier higher than the Xerox.

Special Features

When equipped with a logo font, the Xerox 8700 is capable of printing specially designed forms with the company logo. The font retails for $1,000.

Neither IBM machine has the capability to print the company logo. Current practice is to use outside contractors for these forms. Last month's charges for forms with the company's logo were $235, and demand for these forms has been increasing.

Spreading the cost of the logo font over the 5-year estimated life span of the Xerox 8700 would bring this cost to approximately $16.70 a month. Factoring in this amount, plus the outside charges for the IBMs, brings monthly costs to the following levels:

IBM 1403	IBM 3211	Xerox 8700
$7,303	$7,217	$7,217

Operator time

Table 2 shows the number of operator hours required to produce 200,000 and 300,000 pages per month on the three copiers.

With operator time down to 5 hours a day on the Xerox 8700 at 200,000 pages per month, a full-time operator could spend the remaining 3 hours each day inputting data. Present workloads for input operators already include overtime.

Table 2 also shows that only the Xerox 8700 would avoid operator overtime at the likely 300,000 pages per month output volume.

Table 2   Daily Operator Time Required

ITEM	IBM 1403($)	IBM 3211($)	Xerox 8700($)
For 200,000 pages /month	10.6 h	7.8 h	5 h
For 300,000 pages/month	15.9 h	11.7 h	7.5 h

Conclusions and Recommendation

The Xerox 8700 is lowest in operating costs when the factors of paper cost increases and logo form printing are included in the totals. The Xerox 8700 has the additional advantage of higher printing speed. Faster printing would free operators to help reduce overtime.

I recommend the company lease the Xerox 8700 beginning with the next fiscal quarter.

6 Progress Report

When you are in the middle of a project, particularly one that is lengthy, complex, or collaborative, it's a good idea to have a progress report, or, sometimes, interim or status reports. They range from simple fill-in-the-blank approaches to lengthy discussions, but all progress reports meet the same broad purposes.

Progress reports can check that you're keeping on schedule, record work accomplished over a specified period, convince a client, sponsor, or adviser that your work is on track and on schedule, and assure readers that there will be no surprises at the project's end. Usually, a progress report might include:

- Work completed.
- Future work.
- Problems.
- Correction.
- Schedule status.
- Budget status.

Here is an example of a short progress report in the form of a memo.

BLICKLE GRAIN DRYER CO.

To: G. I. Smith **Date:** 11 August, 2016
From: M. O. Eddy **Reference:** CD 500B
Subject: Progress Report on Energy Conservation Devices for Grain Dryers

1. Work completed (in %)

Device	No. 1	No. 2	No. 3
Design	100	100	100
Detail	100	100	100
Prototype/models	100	100	100
Construction	100	100	100

2. Work to be completed (in %)

Device	No. 1	No. 2	No. 3
Construction	0	20	40
Test	100	100	100
Pro-tests changes	100	100	100

3. Work performed this week

We transported device No.1 to the test site. It will be ready to schedule for preliminary tests on the layer-dryer when the corn harvest starts in late September. The construction of device No.2 for batch dryers is progressing smoothly.

4. Variance from schedule

The construction of device No.3 for continuous flow dryers is about five days behind schedule. A foundry error made it necessary to scrap one of the aluminum castings used in the hot air recycling mechanism.

5. Correction of variance

A new casting has been made and we have arranged with our machine shop to process it immediately upon delivery. Our prospects of meeting the schedule for it looks good right now.

6. Budget status

Amount spent this week	$2,676
Amount authorized	$35,000
Amount spent to date	$15,170
Current balance	$19,830

Exercises

I. Fill in the blanks.

1. Reports also help _____ and _____ find more efficient methods of production, raise profits, develop new _____ or _____, and meet social and environmental responsibilities.
2. People produce a number of different types of reports, such as _____, _____, _____, _____, _____, and _____.
3. When composing a report, first _____ in writing the report. That purpose also reflects the reader's reason for reading the report.
4. Although reports can take many forms, most contain the following major sections: _____, _____, body, ending and _____.
5. A report should be _____, _____, _____, _____, _____, and _____ in terms of writing style.

II. Drafting.

Your college is planning to improve the educational facilities. You are asked to conduct an investigation of the educational facilities in your college.

At the end of the investigation, you and your partner need to compose a report which will be submitted to the dean of your college. The improvement will be based on the result of the report.

Please discuss with your partner about the following questions:

1. What matters should be included in the investigation?
2. What subtitles should be included in the outline of the report?

Chapter 6

Business Proposal

> **Brainstorm**
>
> (1) When the Students' Union or your class want to organize some activities, have you ever tried to propose something? What are the difficulties in offering your suggestions at that moment?
>
> (2) In your opinion, how can people assess the feasibility of a proposal?

扫描二维码
浏览视频
"Introduction to Proposal Writing"

Proposals are made all the time. People may propose by saying "Why don't we…?" or "Why don't you…?" These causal suggestions remain undeveloped because a major flaw in the proposal is quickly apparent.

Yet, the "Why don't we…?" impulse has been the starting point for many successful projects and occasionally for historic breakthroughs. The impulse comes from the perception of a problem or the more general feeling that things are not as good as they could be stated in a more positive way. It comes from recognizing an opportunity.

The written proposal is a full description of a problem and its solutions. It gives enough details to allow the reader to evaluate the merits of the proposed action. It also attempts to sell an idea and therefore uses the strategies of any effective sales message. A proposal is an offer to provide a product, or service or to do some kind of work to solve a problem. It offers clear-cut benefits and helps the reader to act on the proposal. It is a common planning and evaluation tool in organizations facing problems or looking for opportunities. By requiring systematic study of an existing situation and of actions that might create an improvement, the proposal pulls together many of the facts needed to make a decision. And because it usually travels up the chain of command, a well-prepared proposal can bring recognition and advancement to the author. Even if the proposal is not accepted, the work you put into it is likely to pay off in a clearer understanding of the situation you have studied.

There are two main purposes for writing a business proposal. The most important, is to serve as a guide during the life of your business. It is the blueprint of your business and will serve to keep you on the right track. To be of value, your proposal must be kept current. If you spend time on planning ahead, many pitfalls will be avoided and needless frustrations will be eliminated. Second, the business proposal is a requirement if you are planning to seek loan funds. It will provide potential lenders with detailed information on all aspects of the company's past and current operations and provide future projections.

A proposal can be a simple one-page document written by one person for one reader. It can be a multivolume document composed by a team of 300 people and read by 20 or 30 evaluators. And it can be something in between. Broadly conceived, proposals document ways to make the world a better place.

The purpose of a proposal is to show how, in a particular context, the world can be made better. In some cases, a proposal is a written document prepared in application for funding. For example:

A nurse proposes the implementation of an improved triage system in an emergency room.

An engineer proposes an oil filtering system to recycle old oil and thus save money in both purchasing and disposal.

Consultants write proposals that show how they would prepare an environmental impact statement for a project.

Furniture companies write a bid (proposal) to sell desks and chairs to universities.

Proposals may also be classified as internal or external to an organization. An internal proposal is addressed to a higher level within the organization and suggests changes and improvements. The external proposal is written on behalf of the organization and represents an offer to another organization to solve a problem or fill a need in a particular way for a specified compensation.

Most internal proposals aimed below the executive management level are categorized as informal submissions; internal proposals to senior management and external proposals are presented as formal documents.

Proposals are communication tool enabling applicants to express the needs of their local community, the value of the proposed services, and the expertise and capability of the applicant agency to the funder. The following sections are the optional sections included as standard format in most proposals.

- ***Cover Letter, title page, and/or abstract.*** It introduces the project and agency to the funder. The first page, or the cover of your proposal, will be the cover sheet. It serves as the title page of your proposal, and should contain the following information: ①Name of company. ②Company address. ③Company phone number. ④Logo. ⑤Names, titles, addresses, phone numbers. ⑥Month and year in which the proposal is issued. ⑦Name of preparer.

- ***Executive summary.*** It is a statement of the proposal in miniature, although it is sometimes written after the finish of the proposal. It identifies the problem, explains the approach, and justifies its approach as the best one.
- ***Needs statement.*** It describes the community to be served and the problem or need being addressed by the proposal.
- ***Project description.*** It includes goals and objectives and provides details about the implementation plan.
- ***Evaluation plan.*** It explains the measurement procedures that will be used to determine if goals and objectives have been met.
- ***Budget request.*** It itemizes the expenditures of the project and includes a rationale or budget justification for the expenses.
- ***Applicant capability.*** It demonstrates the applicant's past performance and ability to accomplish the proposed project.
- ***Future funding plans.*** It indicates the plan to continue the project beyond the requested funding period.
- ***Letters of support.*** Letters reflect community support for the proposed project from program recipients, community leaders, agencies, schools, and/or religious organizations.
- ***Appendix materials.*** These may include an audited financial statement, insurance documentation, or any other documentation required by the funder.

1. Collaborative Work

Proposals are most often written by more than one person. If the proposal is being written by partnership, there may be one administrator and a grant-writer from the lead agency and one or two together from participating agencies. If a sole agency is writing the proposal, a grant-writer, an executive director, a program director, a program staff may be involved in the writing, whatever the configuration, there is usually one main writer. This "point person" pulls it all together into one style, ensures that all of the extra materials are gathered up for inclusion into the grant, and makes certain that the grant application is in the format required by the funder.

When writing the proposal, you may have one pile for the data related to the program, another for work plans from your agency and other agencies if you are collaborating, another for budgets from each of those agencies, and still another for support letters or other documentation from each participating agency. The best grant-writer works with an editor, who helps to ensure that the main ideas in the proposal are clearly stated and the proposal is internally consistent. All of the numerical totals in budgets should be double-checked by the editor as well. The editor also double-check that all attachments are included and the proposal is assembled accurately.

2. Managing the Collaborative Effort
1) Agreeing on the Core Concept

The first responsibility of the proposal team is to agree on the proposal's core concept. Otherwise, the team can run into trouble when members approach the project with varying ideas about the proper outcome, varying levels of enthusiasm, and varying commitments to a task that is often not their main responsibility. A clear sense of purpose and good leadership help the team overcome these problems, and prevent team members from duplicating each other's work.

2) Assigning Tasks

Team members usually form into three subgroups, each performing a major proposal function: marketing, technology, and communication.

Briefly, the marketing group begins the process by initiating or maintaining contact with the client or customers and then identifying the problem to be addressed. Next the group turns the problem to technical group who determines whether the organization is the right one to solve it, and how to solve it. Finally, the communication group writes the proposal.

The technical team consists of various experts, including scientists, engineers, lawyers, accountants, or other professionals. They provide the major content of the document. Due to their professional ability, some of them may establish the detailed statement of the problem, the core idea, product, or service, or the method for implementing the idea. The financial experts may deal with financial matters, create the budget, and the lawyers may prepare legal commentary, etc. finally, the communication team interweaves the marketing and technical efforts to articulate the clear, persuasive message, and supervises the design and production of the proposal.

3) Developing the Final Program and Budget

The program offerings are listed under the goal areas. The amount of funding requested is placed alongside each program offering. The column is totalled, and, invariably, the budget needed exceeds the funder's allocation. Using the ranking system developed by the community and service providers, the whole group makes the decisions about what will stay as proposed, what might be adjusted, and what will be eliminated from the proposal.

This process allows true collaboration to occur. In many instances, agencies are able to contribute some services "in kind", meaning that they will not receive money for these services but will instead pay for the services they are tying into the proposal.

3. Common Elements of a Proposal

Proposals may have various elements, due to the purpose of writing and the complexity of the problem. Here is an example of proposal, which is also called business plan.

1. Executive summary
2. Product or service
3. Management team
4. Market and competition
5. Marketing and sales
6. Business system and organization
7. Timing
8. Opportunities and risks
9. Financial planning and financing

Some questions will help you produce successful content in the frame of proposal.

Questions for writing executive summary

1. What is your business idea? In what way does it fulfill the criterion of uniqueness?
2. Who are your target customers?
3. What is the value for those customers?
4. What market volume and growth rates are you forecasting?
5. What distribution channels will you use?
6. What competitive environment do you face?
7. What partnerships would you like to enter into?
8. What additional stages of development are needed?
9. How much investment is necessary?
10. What are the sales, costs and profit situations?
11. What long term goals have you set?
12. What opportunities and risks do you face?

Questions for writing about product / service

1. Which end consumer will you address?
2. What are the customer's needs?
3. What customer value does your product/service provide?
4. What is the nature of your innovation?
5. What partnerships are necessary to achieve full customer value?
6. What competitor products are under development?
7. Is your product/service permitted by law?
8. What are the prerequisites for development and manufacturing?
9. What stage of development has your product/service reached?
10. Do you need patents or licenses?
11. What further development steps do you plan to take? What milestones must be reached?

Questions for writing about market and competition

> 1. How is the industry developing?
> 2. Which factors are decisive for success in your industry?
> 3. What role do innovation and technological advances play?
> 4. What market volume (value and amount) do you estimate for your individual market segments over the next five years?
> 5. What will influence growth in the market segments?
> 6. What is your estimate of current and future profitability of the individual market segments?
> 7. What market shares do you hold in each market segment? Which segments are you targeting?
> 8. How will you segment the market?
> 9. Who are your target customer groups?
> 10. What customer examples can you give?
> 11. How much do you depend on large customers?
> 12. What are the key buying factors for customers?
> 13. What role do service, consulting, maintenance, and retail sales play?
> 14. What are the barriers to market entry?
> 15. How do the competitors operate? Which strategies are pursued?
> 16. What market share does your competitor have in the various market segments?
> 17. What target groups do your competitors address?
> 18. How profitable are your competitors?
> 19. What are your competitors' marketing strategies?
> 20. What distribution channels do your competitors use?
> 21. How sustainable will your competitive edge be? Why?
> 22. How will competitors react to your market launch? How will you respond to this reaction?

4. Get Started
1) Writing the Needs Statement

The primary focus of a proposal is to improve conditions or address a problem existing. You begin the proposal development process with an understanding of the need or problem as the basis for conceptualizing your proposed program or intervention. Likewise, when you begin writing the proposal, the needs statement is typically the first part completed. It provides a convincing case regarding the extent and magnitude of the need or problem in your community, and it describes the problem in terms of how people directly or indirectly experience it.

The term *needs statement* is generally used in seeking funding for programs or services, whereas problem statement usually applies to research-oriented proposals. The purpose of the needs statement is to identify the compelling conditions, problems, or issues that are leading you to propose a plan of action.

This section of your proposal does not describe your approach to address the need or problem; rather, it provides a strong rationale for why support should be provided. The needs statement is rooted in factual information. The conceptualization of your proposal is guided by an understanding of the needs or problems not only at the level at which you provide services but also in the larger context of the community, sate or nation.

An effective needs statement does four things:

- It uses supportive evidence to describe clearly the nature and extent of the need/problem facing those you plan to serve.
- It illuminates the factors contributing to the problem or the circumstances creating the need.
- It identifies current gaps in services or programs.
- Where applicable, it provides a rationale for the transferability of the "promising approaches" or "best practices" you are now proposing.

The needs statement makes clear what is occurring that requires prompt attention before conditions worsen, provides an explanation as to why the problem or need exists, and identifies some of the strategies used in other settings that have the potential for addressing the problem or need in your area. You must thoroughly understand the significance of the needs section, as it provides the underpinnings of the remainder of the proposal. As stated before, the needs section is not the place in the proposal to propose your particular "solution" or project. Rather, it lays the foundation for your particular solution to emerge as one that is responsive to the need.

Ideally, the needs statement is comprehensive in its treatment of the need/problem, but is not boring. Be judicious in your selection of data, and use data that most pointedly tell the story of those you intend to serve.

Needs Statement

The majority of families are only one paycheck away from homelessness. This fact is all too real. The majority of the homeless _____ (defined as those without semi-permanent or permanent shelter) in _____ (your county) are single mothers with children repressing the fastest-growing segment of the homeless population.

(It begins with a factual opening sentence that states the topic and captures the attention of the reader.)

In fact, in _____ (year) the homelessness rate in _____ (your county) was _____, which exceeded the state rate of _____ and the national rate of _____ in the same year (source of data).

Although lower than the state and national rates of _____ and _____ respectively, _____ (your county) has seen a significant increase in homelessness over the past 5 years and, without intervention, will meet and exceed national rates within the next _____ years (source of data).

(It compares the local level data to the state and national data. If the incidence of the problem is greater than the state or national rates, your job is easy. If your rate is so low as to make your application noncompetitive, you may need to find some unique reason why your community's problem is significant. For example, you may have higher crime rates as a result of homelessness, or you may have more health problems within the homeless population. Contrast the high incidence of the problem to the low incidence of homelessness to make a stronger case.)

A variety of conditions may ultimately lead to homelessness. Of the homeless population, _____% are mentally ill and unemployed; _____% have experienced the loss of a job; _____% have recently divorced; and _____% are addicted to drugs or alcohol (source of data). The top reason for job loss in the past year was personal health problems, including depression, followed by poor work performance, a lack of job-related skills, absenteeism, and health problems with other family members. In most cases, homelessness does not happen all at once. The family uses all available resources to maintain housing and often has 1 to 3 months of financial struggle before ending up on the streets.

(It accounts for each of the factors that cause the problem. Thus, a discussion of barriers to resolving this problem can also be included. For example, the stigma associated with homelessness may be so great as to cause people to delay seeking assistance, or the clients themselves may have attitudes or beliefs that prevent them from benefiting from assistance.)

The problem of homelessness exacts a significant toll on the homes person and family. Children who are homeless are often uprooted from their schools and their friends, suffer from poor nutrition, and lack even the most basic of preventive care services, such as immunizations.

Once an individual is homeless, the demands on community resources are great. The Government Accounting Office has estimated that it costs taxpayers approximated $35,000 per homeless family per year to provide for the family's basic needs. In a study by _____ (source of data), it was shown that timely intervention targeted at a family in crisis costs approximately $15,000 per year, a savings of over half the cost of delayed intervention! The intervention resulted not only in significant financial savings but also in fewer days lost from school and improved health outcomes among holes children.

> *(An analysis of the impact of the need may present the significance/benefits of the proposal. It can show that the proposed project is cost-effective and it reduces negative consequences and assures future benefits.)*
>
> Several promising strategies have been developed to address the problem of homelessness. The first is the Homeless Project based in Seattle, Washington (source of data). This project targeted a subset of homeless drug-abusing adults and offered treatment incentives and comprehensive services. The program helped over 67% of its participants kick the drug habit, and after a year, 87% of those were employed.
>
> *(It references the particular theoretical and practical program components that will be effective in addressing the need. It also discusses the pros and cons of particular strategies, and considers the unique needs of your participants.)*

2) Writing Goals and Objectives

The two terms "goals" and "objectives" are often used interchangeably. We need to distinguish between them for better elaboration. Goals respond to identified needs or problems and are statements of the ultimate mission or purpose of the program. They represent an ideal or "hoped-for" state of the desired change. Objectives represent the desired and measurable outcomes or results that are essential for achieving the ultimate goals.

For example:

Goals may be: *"to eliminate child abuse"* or *"to prevent domestic violence"*.

Objectives may be: *"to improve family functioning by 25%"* or *"to decrease by 10% the cases of reported domestic violence in the city"*.

As can be seen in these examples, goals are ambitious statements! They are the desired state of things. They are not generally attainable over the short term, yet they help us to keep our focus and communicate the project clearly to others.

Most proposals identify one, two or, at the most, three goals. However, objectives are the expected results of the actions taken to attain the goal. They provide the "promise" of what will be achieved over the course of the funding period. Objectives are specific, achievable, measurable statements about what is going to be accomplished within a certain time frame. Typically, three to four objectives are derived from each goal and are defined more narrowly because you are predicting that you will accomplish certain things within an agreed-on time period.

It is wise to develop objectives for each type of change expected and for each target group. For example, with the goal "to eliminate child abuse and neglect," some objectives may be targeted at parents, some at teachers, and some at the community. In collaboration, agencies can develop objectives that are agency specific or shared with collaborative partners. Developing shared objective within a collaborative agency be especially challenging because organizations must collectively take responsibility for the desired results. Shared objectives require a certain level of trust between agencies.

There are two types of objectives: process objectives and outcome objectives.

Process objectives describe the expected improvements in the operations or procedures, quantify the expected change in the usage of services or methods, and identify how much service will be received. Process objectives do not indicate the impact on the program recipients; rather, they are formulated because the activities involved in implementation are important to the overall understanding of how a problem or need gets addressed. They help to provide insight into experimental, unique, and innovative approaches or techniques used in a program. Process objectives are usually designed to increase knowledge about how to improve the delivery of services.

Outcome objectives specify a target group and identify what will happen to them as a result of the intervention or approach. Outcomes may depict a change in one or more levels, such as client, program, agency, system, cross-systems, or community. Changes may occur in multiple areas. Well-stated outcome objectives provide: ①A time frame. ②The target group (possibly identified in terms of their age, gender, and ethnicity, if applicable). ③The number of program recipients. ④The expected measurable results or benefits. ⑤The geographic location or service locale.

The following example shows how a single goal can lead to several process objectives and outcome objectives.

An example of goal statement

> - **Goal:** To prevent drug use among young people by promoting their academic success and emotional well-being.
>   - **Process objectives:**
>   ① To form a coalition of 10 youth-serving agencies in order to develop a comprehensive plan for providing after-school activities by June 30, 20XX.
>   ② To establish a multilingual teen drug prevention hotline with a corp of 100 volunteers by June 30, 20XX.
>   ③ To develop a multimedia drug abuse prevention campaign targeted to junior high school students and their parents by June 30, 20XX.
>   - **Outcome objectives:**
>   ① One hundred at-risk junior high school students attending the after-school peer counseling program will increase by 60% their knowledge about the dangers of drug and alcohol use by June 30, 20XX.
>   ② One hundred and twenty-five junior high school students who are academically at risk will show a 30% improvement in their reading and math scores by June 30, 20XX.

> ③ One hundred and fifty parents will increase by 60% their knowledge about effective communication techniques for teaching their children about decision making, goal setting, and the dangers and lure of drugs by June 30, 20XX.
>
> ④ One hundred parents will increase their involvement with their children's school by 10% by June 30, 20XX.

3) Developing the Implementation Plan

The implementation plan is the "nuts and bolts" of the proposal: it provides a clear account of what you plan to do, who will do it, and in what time frame the activities will be accomplished. This section is the next step after writing the goals and objectives for it explains to the funder how the objectives will be achieved. The design of your program should generate confidence that it is the most feasible approach for addressing the need/problem.

A variety of activities and resources will be needed to achieve program outcomes. The resources include personnel (staff, volunteers, program recipients, community groups, other organizations), non-personnel (equipment, facilities, materials, supplies), and other funds needed.

Preparatory activities are the start-up activities or general tasks necessary to get the program underway. With each task it is also useful to identify the person responsible for accomplishing the activity and to estimate the time needed for completion. Although the type of preparatory activities will vary depending on the nature of your program, the following items are typical.

- Developing staffing plans.
- Selecting site/facilities.
- Ordering special equipment.
- Selecting products or materials.
- Setting up interagency agreements and collaboration plans.
- Building community linkages and partnerships.
- Developing outreach strategies and approaches to involving program participants.
- Setting up evaluation mechanisms.

In general, human services programming can be grouped into five major categories: ① Training or education. ② Information development and dissemination. ③ Counseling and other support services. ④ Provision of resources or changing conditions. ⑤ Advocacy and systems change. The following questions are designed to assist you in identifying the kinds of activities that might be required to conduct programs in the five major categories.

Example 1: Training or education program
- *What are the training or educational objectives?*
- *What will be the content of the presentations?*

- What strategies or techniques will be most effective with the population?
- Who will conduct the training? What criteria will be used to select trainers?

Example 2: Information development and dissemination
- Who is the targeted audience?
- What will be the content and format?
- Who will develop it?
- Which group will review before distribution to determine the effectiveness and appropriateness?
- What dissemination strategies will be used?

In addition to a description of project activities, funders typically desire to see a schedule of those activities. A visual display of the action plan provides the reader with a real sense of when different phases of the project will be undertaken. It also helps to generate confidence in your ability to effectively carry out the plan.

A variety of techniques can be used to present the project's timetable. One of the most common is a Gantt chart: ①List the major activities and tasks. ②Estimate the amount of time to be expended on each activity or task. ③Determine how the activity is spread across a time period. The time period is typically divided into months or quarters, and an activity's beginning and end points are depicted with row bars, X's, or similar markings. Generally, activities are listed in the order in which they will be accomplished (a foreword sequence).

The cost of running a project is expressed in a budget. The budget tells how much it will cost and how the money is to be spent. The demands for accountability and justification of resources are requiring different ways of viewing and categorizing funds. It will be further complicated by multiple funding sources for a single project.

There are different types of budgets, such as line item budgets and performance or functional budgets. A simplified version is presented in Table 6-1.

Table 6-1   A Line Item Budget

Budget Category	Total Budget Request
Personnel	$41,500
Supplies and materials	$15,250
Printing	$7,395
Facilities	$3,650
Equipment	$1,650
Project Total	$69,445

If your proposal is a business plan, remember to produce a financial planning. There are some minimum requirements of a financial planning, besides the budget tables. You need to offer a cash flow calculation (liquidity planning), income statement, balance sheet. Then there should be forecasts over three to five years, at least one year beyond the point of breaking even, which is beyond the generation of positive cash flow. A detailed financial planning for the first two years (monthly or quarterly), thereafter annually should be made. All figures must be based on reasonable assumptions.

Proposals are written in a formal writing style. Unlike a research paper in which you use footnotes or endnotes to cite references, the references are usually incorporated into the body of the text.

Formal writing style requires that you write to the most intelligent of audiences and eliminate informal references or comments such as *"I think"* or *"It seems to me that..."* For the most part, the reviewer of the proposal will be a professional in the field who is well educated and experienced on the issue. You will be expected to use professional terminology appropriately.

A proposal prepared for many foundations or corporations will often be much less complex than one prepared for the federal or state government. Some funders may require the proposal to be only three to six pages in length. Typically, the proposal is written in a less technical and more journalistic style, as the reader is more likely to be an educated "generalist" and not a specialist in the field. It is recommended that in these proposals, the writer avoids the use of professional jargon, as it interferes with the reader's overall understanding of the proposal.

In all cases, the final proposal should be clean and free of spelling or grammatical errors. It should be visually pleasing, with consistent section headers and typefaces. Charts, tables, graphs, and other illustrations can enhance the impact of the proposal and are now widely used. Avoid using shading or color graphs that do not copy well, as a poor copy will detract from your proposal.

How a proposal is designed, especially at the level of subtitles, depends on what kind of venture is envisioned and what the proposal should accomplish. If a proposal is being written for a startup, for example, it will necessarily have a different structure than one aims to launch an existing company into a new segment.

Despite such differences, business proposals have a number of things in common. They are to provide a clear and comprehensive evaluation of the opportunities and risks posed by the operation. This is no small task, and completing it will require careful attention to certain standards of design and content. The following suggestions and guidelines should help you make your proposal successful.

A good business proposal impresses with its clarity. Readers should be able to find suitable answers to their questions. It should be easy for readers to find the topic they are particularly interested in. This means the business plan must have a clear structure to enable readers to maneuver and choose what they would like to read.

It is not the volume of analysis and data, but rather the organization of the statements and a concentration on the essential arguments that will persuade your readers. Any topic that could be of interest to the reader should therefore be discussed fully, but concisely.

A proposal is not read in the presence of the author, who could then answer questions and provide explanations. For this reason, the text must be unambiguous and speak for itself. Each plan should thus be presented to a test audience if at all possible before it is finally submitted. Competition coaches for example, can help weed out confusing passages or indicate areas still in need of editing.

A good business proposal convinces with its objectivity. Some people get carried away when they are describing what they feel is a good idea. While there is something to be said for enthusiasm, you should try to keep your tone objective and give the reader a chance to carefully weigh your arguments. A proposal written like glowing advertising copy is more likely to irritate than appeal to your readers, making them suspicious, skeptical or otherwise unreceptive.

Equally dangerous is being too critical of your own project in response to various past miscalculations or mistakes. This will raise questions about your ability and motivation. To the best of your knowledge, the data should be accurate. Weaknesses should never be mentioned without introducing methods to correct them or plans to do so. This does not mean that fundamental weaknesses should be hidden, just that in preparing your plan, you should develop approaches to remedying them, which you then present with clarity.

A good business proposal can be understood by the technical layman. Some entrepreneurs believe that they can impress their readers with profuse technical details, elaborate blueprints, and the small print of an analysis. They are mistaken. Only rarely are technical experts called to evaluate this data carefully. In most cases, a simplified explanation, sketch, or photograph is appreciated. If technical details of the product or manufacturing process must be included, you should put them in the appendix.

A good business proposal is written in one consistent style. Several people usually work together to produce a business plan. In the end, this work must be integrated to avoid creating a patchwork quilt of varying styles and analytical depth. For this reason, it is best to have one person edit the final version.

A good business proposal is your calling card. Finally, your business proposal should have a uniform visual layout. The fonts, for example, should be consistent with the structure and contents, effective graphics should be neatly integrated and perhaps, a header with the (future) company logo used.

Exercises

I. Fill in the blanks.

1. The written proposal is a full description of a problem and its _____. It is an offer to provide a _____, or _____ or to do some kind of work to solve a problem. It offers clear-cut benefits and helps the reader to _____ the proposal.

2. Proposals may also be classified as _____ or _____ to an organization.

3. An effective needs statement does four things:
   1) It uses _____ to describe clearly the nature and extent of the need/problem facing those you plan to serve.
   2) It illuminates the factors contributing to the problem or the circumstances creating the need.
   3) It identifies _____ in services or programs.
   4) Where applicable, it provides a _____ for the transferability of the "promising approaches" or "best practices" you are now proposing.

4. In a proposal, objectives are the _____ of the actions taken to attain the goal. They provide the "promise" of what will be achieved over the course of the funding period. Objectives are specific, achievable, measurable _____ about what is going to be accomplished within a certain time frame.

5. It is recommended that, in these proposals, the writer avoids the use of _____, as it interferes with the reader's overall understanding of the proposal.

II. Discussion.

Please discuss with your partner over the following questions, and write down your answers briefly: How can people assess a proposal? What are the reasons if a proposal is rejected?

Chapter 7

Business Letter

> **Brainstorm**
>
> (1) What are the basic formats of business letters? Define what indented format means.
> (2) Can you make a list of a typical business letter? What requirements should we follow when writing each part?

Business letters may be the longest-existing type of business correspondence and the most traditional way for business communication. Despite the development and expansion of electronic alternatives, letters have remained an important vehicle for both internal and external communication. In most circumstances, they officially represent your company or organization you represent.

Business letter is most representative of business documents whose format is a general instruction to all the other documents. The format of your letter is important and it should follow a certain order.

扫描二维码
浏览视频
"The Key Forms
of Business
Writing-basic
Letter"

1. Elements of Business Letters

A properly structured letter provides clarity for the reader to look for the date, reference number and other elements; meanwhile, the proper structure would earn the recipient's respect. The body itself, structured with an introduction, body and conclusion, creates a purpose and an action for the next step, which shows that you have taken time to write clearly. Therefore, you should know that a traditional business letter, generally, contains the following parts or elements.

(1) Letter head.
(2) Reference and date.
(3) Inside name and address.
(4) Attention line.
(5) Salutation.

(6) Subject line.

(7) Body.

(8) Complimentary close.

(9) Signature.

(10) Enclosure.

(11) Carbon copy notation.

(12) Postscript.

Among the 12 elements, letter head, date, inside address, salutation, body, complementary close and signature are necessary, and the rests are optional.

1) Letter Head

Letter head includes the sender's name, postal address, telephone number, telex number, fax number, cable address, and logo, etc. Usually letter head is printed in the up-center or at the left margin of a letter (Figure 7-1).

Hualian Chemical Products Company
Shenzhen, China
Tel: 67804
Telex: 446834
Fax: (5677) 678008

Figure 7-1 Letter Head

In some countries, letter head contains other details. For example, in the UK, the directors' names of a company are given or icon of products. This is usually a miniature of the products the company manufactures or sells, such as an automobile, a computer or a motorcycle. A glance at the icon will tell you what line of business the firm is in.

2) Reference and Date

In business communication, when firms write to each other, they will give a reference. The reference may include a file number, departmental code or the initials of the signer followed by that of the typist of the letter. These are marked "Our ref:" and "Your ref:" to avoid confusion.

Your ref: JBD/WM

Our ref: WDW/LP

The date line is generally typed two or three lines below the letter head. The date line may start from the left margin, or be centered, or appear on the right-hand side, with the last figure serving as a guide for the right-hand margin.

The date should be typed in one line and generally the week days do not appear.

It is preferably typed in the order of D/M/Y: day, month, and year, because nowadays most computer-processed forms bear a date box in such an order; but, in practice, quite a few people write the date in the M/D/Y order.

The date may be expressed either in cardinals or in ordinals. If you use ordinals, pay special attention to the numerals containing the units *1, 2* and *3*, because when dating a letter, beginners are apt to write *1th, 2th, 3th, 21th, 22th, 23th*, and *31th*, or *11st, 12nd* and *13rd*. To avoid making such mistakes, use cardinals.

English form follows the order of day, month and year while it is the US practice to write in the order of month, day and year. So, 10/2/2016 could be mistaken as either October 2, 2016 or February 10, 2016.

However, since the D/M/Y order is widely used on word-processors, and, since most Europeans write the date in a highly abbreviated form —*1.7.99*—, if you prefer to write the month in numerals, it is always advisable to adopt the D/M/Y order, and express the day, month, and year with two digits. Besides, as we have only twelve months in a year, if the day is 13 or larger, the month can be assuredly expressed in numeral. For example, *13/01* or *01/13* is doubtlessly *January 13*.

In case the date line is typed in the M/D/Y order, then after the day (especially when it is in cardinals) you should use a comma to separate the numerals respectively expressing the day and year (e.g. *January 1, 2016)*.

3) Inside Name and Address

The name and address of the receiver is typed at the left-hand margin about two to four spaces below the date. It appears exactly the same way as on the envelope.

Mr., Mrs., Miss., and Ms—the ordinary courtesy titles are used to address to one person. Mr. for a man, Mrs., Miss. or Ms. for a woman.

e.g. Mr. C. E. Eckersley, Ms. M. C. Mar

After the name, his or her official position should follow, if there is any.

e.g. Mr. C. C. Eckersley, Director

Ms. M. C. Mar, President

Messrs. (abbreviation of Messieurs) is, also a courtesy title, used for partnerships whose firm's name includes a personal element. It is not used when the name carries a courtesy title, as Sir William Dobson & Sons, or when the word "the" forms part of the name, as the Grayson Electrical Co.

4) Attention Line

Attention line is used when the writer of a letter addressed to an organization wishes to direct the letter to a specific individual or section of the firm. It generally follows the inside address.

e.g. Attention: Mr. Smith   Attention: The Sales Manager

5) Salutation

Salutation is the complimentary greeting with which the writer opens his letter. Its form depends on the writer's relationship with the receiver. The customary formal greeting in a business letter is "Dear Sir" or "Dear Madam" used for addressing one person; and "Dear Sirs" "Dear Mesdames" or "Gentlemen" for addressing two or more people. If the receiver is known to the writer personally, warmer greeting "Dear Mr. Sb." is preferred.

Salutation is usually typed three spaces below the inside address of the attention line, and followed by a comma for "Dear Sir" "Dear Sirs", and a colon for "Gentlemen". Table 7-1 shows common salutation.

Table 7-1　Common Salutation

Addressee	British English	American English
Company or institution	Dear Sirs,	Dear Gentlemen:
Man (name unknown)	Dear Sir,	
Woman (name unknown)	Dear Madam,	
Name and gender unknown	Dear Sir or Madam,	
Man	Dear Mr. Blair,	the same as British English
Married woman or widow	Dear Mrs. Blair,	
Unmarried woman	Dear Miss Blair,	
Woman (the modern way)	Dear Ms. Blair,	
Woman (marital status unknown)	Dear Ms. Blair,	
Married couple	Dear Mr. and Mrs. Blair,	
Friend/acquaintance	Dear Blair,	

6) Subject Line

Subject line is actually the general idea of a letter. It is inserted between the salutation and the body of the letter either at the left-hand margin for fully-blocked letter form or centrally over the body for other forms. It calls the receiver's attention to the topic of the letter.

A subject line is often typed either in capital and small or in all-capital letters, beginning with the word **"Subject"** **"Re"** **"Underlined"** or **"Capitalized"**. Each is followed by a colon. Examples can be seen as follows.

Re: Late Delivery of Order 123

Subject: Your order No. C317/8 dated 12th March 2014

Underlined: Sale Contract No. 234

Capitalized: SALE CONTRACT NO. 234

7) Body

This is the main part of the letter. It expresses the writer's idea, opinion, purpose and wish, etc. It should be carefully planned. The body of the letter usually contains the actual message of the sender in three parts.

(1) Opening part. It is the introductory part of the letter. In this part, attention of

the reader should be drawn to the previous correspondence, if any.

(2) Main part. This part usually contains the subject matter of the letter. It should be precise and written in clear words and to the point.

(3) Concluding part. It contains a statement of the sender's intentions, hopes or expectations concerning the next step to be taken. Further, the sender should always look forward to getting a positive response.

For very short letters, you may adopt double-line-spacing except for your correspondent's name and address for which single-line-spacing should always be used.

8) Complimentary Close

Complimentary close is a polite way of ending a letter. It appears two lines below the last line of the text. Its alignment varies with the format of the letter. In block letters, the complimentary close appears flush with the left margin. In modified and indented letters, it appears in the center, flush with the right margin. "Yours sincerely" "Respectfully yours", or "Respectfully" are complimentary closes for very formal letters, "Best wishes" "Kindest regards" "Regards" "Best regards", and "Cordially" for informal letters. "Sincerely yours" is the American style while "Yours sincerely" is the British style.

The complimentary close should convey the level of formality and degree of personal feeling that the writer has for the reader.

What is more, it must be in accordance with the salutation.

Salutation	Complementary Close
Dear Sir/Dear Madam	Yours faithfully
Dear Mr. Raj	Yours sincerely
My Dear Akbar	Yours very sincerely

The complimentary close, when used, must never be separated from the substance of a letter or carried to a separate sheet. The letter must be scrapped and retyped—leaving narrower spaces to retype the letter within one sheet of paper or rearranging the letter with some portion of the body carried over to the next sheet.

When using continuous sheets, plain paper of the same quality as the letter head must be used and typed with a heading to show:

- The number of the sheet (in the center of the page).
- The name of your correspondent (on the left-hand side).
- The date of the letter (on the right-hand side).

9) Signature

It is common to type the name of the writer's firm or company immediately below complimentary close. Then the person who dictates the letter should sign his name, by hand and in ink below it. Since hand-written signatures are illegible, the name of the signer is usually typed below the signature, and followed by his job title or position.

The followings are examples of signing a business letter

(a)
                                      Yours faithfully,
THE NATIONAL TRANSPORT CO.

Wang Dawei

Wang Dawei

Manager

(b)
                                        Yours truly,
for THE OVERSEAS CO., LTD.

W. Black

W. Black

President

10) Enclosure

If something is enclosed, note it below the signature.

11) Carbon Copy Notation

When copies of the letter are sent to others, type c. c. below the signature at the left margin.

c. c. The Osaka Chamber of Commerce   c. c. Mr. G Well

12) Postscript

If the writer wishes to add something he forgot to mention or for emphasis, he may add his postscript two spaces below the carbon copy notation.

P. S. The samples will be mailed to you tomorrow.

2. Formats of Business Letters

When you work for a company, that business is likely to have a preference for a certain business letter style. In fact, in some cases, a template is used to prepare correspondence. That ensures all letters have a uniform appearance.

There are three basic ways of setting out business letters.

- The block format.
- The modified block format.
- The indented format.

1) The Block Format

The block format is also known as the full block format, and it is the most common format nowadays. In this format everything, from the date to the signature, is ranged on the left-hand margin. There is no indenting; new paragraphs are identified by leaving a line space. The following is a business letter in the block format. It is popular because it is quicker. No time-consuming layout is required—everything starts at one margin.

扫描二维码
浏览视频
"Creating a Modified Block Letter"

扫描二维码
浏览视频
"Letter Style—Block and Variation"

Sample 1: A Business Letter in the Block Format

Blyco F&B Group B.V.
Ossterstra 27524DZ Enscgede
The Netherlands
Tel: 53-8774
Telex: 45635
Fax: 53-333117

Your ref: C9246
Our ref: bwbw

Date: April 24, 2016

Xi'an F&B Corp
108 Lianhu Road
Xi'an, Shanxi, China

Dear Sirs,

    Thank you for your letter of April 18, 2016. We are a company that is engaged in importing food stuff from your country, although not from Xi'an.

    We are interested in your contacts. Our Purchasing Manager, who is in HK at the moment, will contact you when he returns.

Yours faithfully,
Blyco F&B Group B.V.

J. Kistemaker
J. Kistemaker, Manager

2) The Modified Block Format

    In the modified block format, your address, date (the date can actually go on either the left or the right side), closing, signature, and printed name are all indented to the right half of the page (how far you indent is up to you as long as the heading and the closing are lined up, and use your own discretion and make sure it looks presentable). Here is a business letter in the modified block format.

Sample 2: A Business Letter in the Modified Block Format

Gregory Donaldson
Minoan Inc
247 Madison Ave., Suite 2013
New York, NY 10015

December 3, 2016

Dixie Cleverelle
Savbizcor Ltd
28 Green St., Suite 14
Upstate, NY 10947

Dear Ms. Cleverelle:

    The first shipment of equipment from Savbizcor Ltd has arrived. We are delighted with every piece. Therefore, we decided to make our initial purchase larger than anticipated. I am attaching Purchase Order No. 8930 for additional goods totaling list price $ 700,000.

    Since you already have a copy of procurement guidelines, I shall not attach them to this order. As before, we will establish a letter of credit. Please inform me of shipping dates.

Sincerely,

G. Donaldson

Gregory Donaldson
Chief Procurement Officer

Enclosure: Purchase Order No. 8930

3) The Indented Format

    In the indented format, your address, date (the date can actually go on either the left or the right side), closing, signature, and printed name are all indented to the right half of the page (how far you indent is up to you as long as the heading and the closing are lined up, and use your own discretion and make sure it looks presentable). Also the first line of each paragraph is indented. The indentation of the first line of each paragraph is the only difference between the indented formats and the modified block formats. Here is a business letter written in the indented format.

Sample 3: A Business Letter in the Indented Format

Imperial Stationery Ltd
258 North Hampton Road, Manhasset, Ny 10847
Tel: 53-8774 Telex:45635 Fax: 53-333117

April 24, 2016

Ms. Ashley Nickols
    Savbizcor Ltd
        28 Green St., Suite 11
            Upstate, NY 10947

Dear Ms. Nickols,

    Thank you for ordering 15 cases of premium paper from Imperial Stationery Ltd. We've shipped your order and it should reach you within the next five business days.

    I enclosed your total bill for the above order amounting to $794.85, and the check for $23.85 is your refund. Because you paid in advance, we are giving you 3 percent cash discount and we also are paying for shipping and handling.

    We are pleased to add you to its list of customers. We look forward to your next order.

Sincerely,

J. O'Conelly

Jennifer O'Conelly
Customer Service

Enclosures

Which business letter format should you use? It will depend on whether you are composing a letter on your own or on behalf of your employer. If you are looking for the easiest letter format, the block format is the one for you. All the components that make up the business letter are positioned flush with the left margin and you don't need to stop to think about centering or indenting any portion of the letter. Some people prefer one of the other commonly-used business letter styles. No style is right or wrong, and the style you choose will depend on your personal preferences, since all of the above formats are appropriate for business use. Sometimes the company you work for expects employees to use a specific format. If you have a style template available, it will be easy to position the parts of your letter at the appropriate points without question.

Exercises

I. Read the following badly-written formal business letter and try to finish the exercises 1-4.

Lee's Furniture Mart

62/66 Downtown, Moreville DT23. Tel: 608 0097

The Manager,
Seaview Guest House,
Parade DT12.

Dear Sirs,

    The furniture you ordered has arrived at hour showrooms. Please telephone the undersigned personally to say weather you will collect it or we should deliver it to you; we shall be unhappy with either. Remember we want your money when you get the furniture so have it ready. Your early reply will be appreciated.

Yours sincerely, Manger

---

1. Write down ten faults in the letter.

(1) _____
(2) _____
(3) _____
(4) _____
(5) _____
(6) _____
(7) _____
(8) _____
(9) _____
(10) _____

2. Rewrite the letter in full, with all ten faults corrected.

3. Answer the following questions.
(1) Why is it so important for the appearance of a business letter to be attractive?
_____
_____

(2) What is "indentation" and why do some letter-writers use it?
_____
_____

4. Choose the best answer.
(1) The addressee of a business letter is _____.
   A. the person or organization from which it is received
   B. the person or organization on behalf of which it is written
   C. the person or organization to whom it is to be sent
   D. the person who signs it
(2) The greeting "Dear Sir or Madam" needs to match with the closing "____".
   A. Yours faithfully
   B. Yours sincerely
   C. Faithfully to you both
   D. Yours truly
(3) The first paragraph of a business letter usually _____.
   A. contains only one sentence
   B. states what the writer wants the addressee to do
   C. starts with the addressee's name
   D. gives the reason why the letter has been written
(4) The term "justification" in relation to a business letter means _____.
   A. that the writer has good reason for the facts contained in it
   B. that it contains all the proof necessary to convince the reader
   C. that it only just fits on one sheet of paper
   D. that all lines containing sufficient words end at the right-hand margin

(5) A prefix _____.
   A. is a senior boy or girl at school
   B. is added to the front of a word to form a new word
   C. involves the use of glue or an adhesive
   D. is added at the end of a word to form a new word

II. Improve the following letter in which some parts of the layout are inappropriate.

INTEGRATED COMPUTER TECHNOLOGY CO., LTD.
Room 808, Kyo-Won-Kong-Jea 35-2 Yeoido
Young Dung Po
Seoul
Republic of Korea
Tel: 822-782-4641　Fax: 822-785-4245
16 June 2016　　　　　　　　　　　　　KJ: rh
Enclosures 2
CC: Kim Sang-Chul
　　Moon Young-Seung
Subject: Integrated Circuit Boards

Dear Dr Brenda Yeoh

　　We have just received your order for 400 integrated circuit boards (item No. KR10779)

　　Unfortunately, these circuit boards are no longer produced as they have been replaced by our Model KR2000, which is cheaper, more reliable and more efficient than the circuit boards you ordered. With this in mind, we imagine that you will be happy to change your order.

　　The prices of the KR2000 and peripheral equipment are as follows:
　　KR2000 integrated circuit board: @$23,200
　　KT200X "Toolkit": @$15,500
　　KC200X connectors: (2 per pack) @$10,000
　　I should be grateful if you could contact me to tell me what you wish us to do.

　　　　　　　　　　　　　　　　　　　　　　　Yours faithfully
　　　　　　　　　　　　　　　　　　　　　　　Kim Jungsup

Chapter 7 Business Letter   85

> For INTERGARATED COMPUTER TECHNOLOGY CO., LTD.
> Attention Dr Brenda Yeoh, PhD
> ATT Computers Corp. Pte Ltd.
> 88 Kitchener Road, #02-15
> Jalan Besar Plaza
> Singapore 208512
> PS Forgot to mention it, but there are lots of bargains in the brochure and prices list which I'm sending you.

III. **Arrange the following items in proper form as they should be set out in a letter.**

(1) Sender's name: China National Light Industrial Products Import & Export Corporation.

(2) Sender's address: 128 Huchiu Road, Shanghai, China

(3) Sender's cable address: INDUSTRY SHANGHAI

(4) Sender's telex address: 33054 INDUS CN

(5) Date: March 23, 2016.

(6) Receiver's name: H. G. Wilkinson Company, Limited

(7) Receiver's address: 245 Lombart Street, Lagos, Nigeria

(8) Salutation used: Dear Sirs,

(9) Subject-matter: Sewing Machines

(10) The Message:
We thank you for your letter of March 16 enquiring for the captioned goods.
The enclosed booklet contains details of all our sewing machines and will enable you to make a suitable selection.

(11) Complimentary close: Yours faithfully.

Part 3

Routine Business Transaction Letter

Chapter 8

Inquiry and Reply

Lead-in: Case Study

Case One

A shoes importer wants to extend his range and gets the information about the exporter from his business connection; please send the inquiry to the exporter to show the desire to establish the business relationship.

Case Two

Hangzhou Textile Import and Export Corporation learns from the Commercial Counselor's Office of the US Embassy that an American company Xinli Textile Inc. intends to have the import of cotton bed-sheets and pillowcases, and the Chinese corporation seizes the opportunity to write a letter to establish the business relationship.

扫描二维码
自学 PPT

1. Establishing Business Relationship

Inquiry means asking, which falls into two catalogues—the first inquiry and the general letter of inquiry. Inquiries mean potential business, so both the buyer and the seller should take great care in writing or replying the letter.

The first inquiry referred as "to establish relationship" comes from both seller and buyer. Companies are more likely to be agreeable to business proposals if they are given every possible detail from the very beginning. To serve the purpose, the first inquiry should include the following information.

(1) How you get the potential partner's name and address.

(2) A self-introduction and/or some indication of the demand in your area for the goods which the supplier (or seller) deals in.

(3) Information as to what the buyer would like the prospective supplier to

provide. Normally the buyer will be interested in a catalogue, a price list, discounts, methods of payments, delivery time, and samples. When the buyer has many points on which information is required, it may be useful to enumerate the inquiry. To ensure smooth and successful transactions, it is also essential to ask for credit information about the prospective dealers such as capital, capacity and character.

(4) A closing sentence to inspire the further relation.

Sample 1: First Inquiry from the Buyer

To: Sales Department
From: Tony Smith
Subject: Establishing Business Relationship

Dear Sirs/Madams,

We have obtained your name and address from Kee & Co., Ltd, and we are writing to ask whether you would be willing to establish business relations with us.
 	
    We have been importers of shoes for many years. At present, we are interested in extending our range and would appreciate your catalogues and quotations.
 	
    If your prices are competitive we would expect to place volume orders with you.
 	
    We look forward to your early reply.
 	
    Yours faithfully,
 	
Tony Smith
Chief Buyer

Sample 2: First Inquiry from the Seller

To: Purchase Department
From: Lily
Subject: Establishing Business Relationship

Dear Sirs/Madams,

From the Commercial Counselor's Office of the US Embassy, we have learned that you wish to import cotton bed-sheets and pillowcases from China.
 	
    We are the leading exporter of textile products in China and have established business relationships with more than 70 countries in the world. Because of the softness and durability, our cotton bed-sheets and pillowcases are rapidly becoming popular.
 	
    You will find the attached catalogue, which may be useful. We have also attached our latest price list for your reference.

Please contact us if you are interested in any of our products.

Look forward to your early reply.

Sincerely yours,

Lily Hu
Export Manager

2. Replies from the Potential Customers

In reply to the first inquiry be sure to first state clearly which letter you refer to, then inform your client whether you are interested in the products or not, if the products are of interest to you, ask for the other details about the goods you need, and lastly end your letter with a complimentary sentence.

Sample 1: Reply from the Seller

To: Tony Smith
From: Ann
Subject: Establishing Business Relationship

Dear Mr. Smith,

Thank you for your letter of the 20th of this month. We shall be glad to enter into business relations with your company.

In compliance with the request, we are sending you, under separate cover, our latest catalogue and price list covering our export range.

Payment should be made by irrevocable and confirmed letter of credit.

If you want to place an order, please fax us.

Yours sincerely,

Ann
Chief Seller

Sample 2: Reply from the Buyer

To: Lily
From: Michel
Subject: Establishing Business Relationship

Dear Lily,

We are glad to receive your letter and would like you to send us details of your various ranges, including sizes, colors and samples of the best quality of material used.

> If they are of the standard we require, we will place a substantial order. We would also like to know if you are offering any trade discounts.
>
> Yours sincerely,
>
> Michel Lee
> General Manager

3. Supplementary Information
1) Channels Approaching to the Prospective Dealers

Channels through which the prospective dealers abroad may be approached are illustrated as follows:

(1) Banks.

(2) A chamber of commerce. A chamber of commerce is an organization of businessmen. One of its tasks is to get business information and to find new business opportunities for its members.

(3) Commercial counselor's office or other commercial institutions at home and abroad.

(4) Advertisements in newspapers, magazines, and the Internet.

(5) Attendance at the export commodities fairs or exhibitions.

(6) The introduction from business connections and mutual visits by trade delegations or groups.

(7) BBS(bulletin board system).

2) Trade Discount

Trade discount is a deduction from the list price allowed by a manufacturer, wholesaler to a retailer, or distributor to a retailer, or one firm to another in the same trade. Usually there are cash discount and quantity discount.

3) Commodity, Merchandise, Cargo and Item

Commodity refers to anything sold for profit. Merchandise is goods bought and sold and always in singular number. Cargo is goods carried by a ship, plane, or vehicle. Item is a single thing on a list or in a catalogue; it is often used to stand for the goods previously mentioned in the letter.

4) Pamphlet, Brochure, Catalogue and Leaflet

Pamphlet is brochure or booklet. Brochure is a small book consisting of a few pages in a paper cover, and advertising material is always in this form. Catalogue is a list, usually in the form of a book of goods for sale with or without prices or pictures. Leaflet is a single sheet or printed paper, sometimes folded to form several pages, containing matter like advertising a product or giving directions on how to use it.

5) Capital, Capacity and Character

Capital means the overall financial worth or assets minus outstanding obligations. Capacity means the ability to promote its line of business as testified by the scope of its establishment and the volume of business actually done. Character means its record of honoring or dishonoring contracts and other obligations.

4. Useful Expressions

(1) *Through the courtesy of the Paris Chamber of Commerce, we have your name as a firm who is interested in doing business with us.*

(2) *Through the courtesy of Mr. White, we are given to understand that you are one of the leading importers of silk in your area.*

(3) *On the recommendation of Messrs. Harvey & Co., we have learned with pleasure the name of your firm.*

(4) *On the recommendation of the Bank of China, we have got to know that you import Chinese textile and cotton piece goods.*

(5) *Your co. has been introduced to us by ABC Trading Corporation.*

(6) *Your co. has been introduced as leading exporter to us by John Smith.*

(7) *We learned from the commercial counselor of our embassy in Ottawa that you deal in general merchandise.*

(8) *We learned from China Daily that you are interested in electrical appliances and want to order immediately.*

(9) *We have your name and address from China Council for the Promotion of International Trade.*

(10) *We are glad to have your name and address from The Journal of Commerce.*

(11) *Your letter of Sept. 8 has been transferred to us for attention from our head office in Beijing.*

(12) *Your inquiry has been forwarded to us for attention from the Commercial Counselor's Office of the Chinese Embassy in Rome.*

(13) *You are recommended to our company by our sister corporation in Shanghai for the new product you are promoting.*

(14) *We specialize in chemical products (cotton piece goods, art and craft goods/arts and crafts/handicraft, straw and willow product, embroideries, porcelain wares, jade carvings, silk flowers, toys and gifts, fat-reducing tea, black tea, tablecloth and bath towels, imitation jewellery, etc.).*

(15) *Messrs. Haruno & Bros. handles electronic products for export.*

(16) *We deal inclusively in textiles.*

(17) *We are a state-operated corporation, handling the export of animal by-products.*

(18) *We are China National Textile Import and Export Corporation, with its headquarters in Beijing.*

(19) *We take the opportunity to introduce our company as exporters dealing exclusively in leather goods.*

(20) *We wish to inform you that we are specialized in the export of arts and crafts.*

(21) *We are pleased to inform you that we handle a wide range of electric fans.*

(22) *We avail ourselves of this opportunity to write to you and see if we can establish business relations with you.*

(23) *We have come to know the name of your corporation and are pleased to write to you in the hope of establishing business relations with you.*

(24) *We are willing to enter into business relations with you on the basis of equality and mutual benefit.*

(25) *Your company has been introduced to us by Smith & Co. Ltd as prospective buyers of Chinese table-cloths. As we deal in the items, we shall be pleased to enter into direct business relations with you.*

(26) *As the item falls within the scope of our business, we shall be pleased to enter into direct business with you.*

(27) *We assure you of the best quality and moderate prices of our goods.*

(28) *We assure you that we shall do our best to promote the business between us.*

(29) *We look forward to your close cooperation in promoting this new product.*

(30) *Please send your catalogue and price list at your earliest convenience.*

Exercises

I. Choose the appropriate word or words to complete the sentences.

1. We introduce ourselves (like, as, for) importers and exporters of light industrial (produce, products), having many years experience in this line of business.
2. We have been (bought, buy, buying) walnut meat from the local commission houses, who (are used to, used to, use to) send us quotations regularly.
3. We take the liberty (to, of, in) writing to you with a hope to get your best offer for Chinese bicycles.
4. It is (gratify, gratifying, grateful) to learn (in, from, through) your letter that you are in a position to supply us with bitter apricot kernels.
5. The import and export business in China is (controlled, handled, done) by the state trading corporations.
6. We have concluded considerable business with Biddle and Sawyer Company (of, in, with, regarding) this line of business.

7. Your prompt (attention, reply, response) to this matter will be very much appreciated.
8. As (regarded, regards) machine tools, we regret to (say, inform) that we are not able to supply for the time being.

II. Arrange the following words and phrases in their proper order.

1. the leading exporters of textiles   we have been informed by
   to extend business to our market   Jameson Garments (Vancouver) Ltd.
   and that you wish   that you are one of

   _____

   _____

2. listed below   for the captioned goods
   we would like to   on the terms and conditions
   have your lowest quotations

   _____

   _____

3. which you recently advertised   please send me
   the line of ultrasonic equipment   in *Electronics*
   the features and costs of   some further information on

   _____

   _____

4. to receive   we are interested in
   a copy of your latest catalogue   and would be pleased
   price list and export terms   importing Chinese furniture

   _____

   _____

5. if you would send us   we would be grateful
   which you can supply   of the goods
   a comprehensive price list   together with some samples

   _____

   _____

III. **Fill in the blanks.**

1. In _____ with our company's growth, to further expand our market, we have decided to establish an office in Dalian.
2. Please be good enough to provide the necessary information _____ us.
3. If your price is competitive, we shall be glad to place a substantial order _____ you.
4. This article is of particular interest _____ us.
5. Our sales contract _____ that the seller shall ship the goods within one month after signing the contract.
6. Will you please provide Mr. Chadwick _____ a letter of recommendation, which you think would be useful?
7. We are gearing our production to your requirements and shall soon be _____ a position _____ offer you substantially.
8. If your price is _____ line _____ the market price, we can take large quantities.
9. There is nothing _____ at present.
10. Enclosed _____ _____ a copy of our price list.
11. He owes his success _____ chance.
12. Through the _____ of a chamber of commerce, we have learned that you are one of those representative importers of electric goods.

IV. **Complete the following sentences in English.**

1. We are given to understand that
   a. 你公司是经营化工产品的国有公司。
   _____
   b. 你公司有意在平等、互利的基础上与我公司建立业务关系。
   _____

2. We are desirous of
   a. 获得你方最近供应出口的商品目录。
   _____
   b. 把你方的新产品介绍给我方的客户。
   _____

3. Please do not hesitate to write us
   a. 关于推销中国水果和干果的任何建议。
   _____
   b. 当你方需要订购手机的时候。
   _____

4. As you know,
   a. 许多外国商人渴望和我们进行贸易。

b. 我们已经和世界上 100 多家商号建立了贸易关系。

5. We are appreciative of
   a. 你方有和我公司建立贸易关系的意向。

   b. 你方愿意到广交会来洽谈业务。

V. Give the English or Chinese equivalents of the followings.

1. 建立贸易关系　　　　　　_____
2. 扩大营业范围　　　　　　_____
3. 最新价目单　　　　　　　_____
4. 主要出口商　　　　　　　_____
5. 生产日期　　　　　　　　_____
6. 供参考　　　　　　　　　_____
7. to place volume orders　　_____
8. in compliance with request　_____
9. trade discount　　　　　　_____
10. irrevocable L/C　　　　　_____
11. chamber of commerce　　 _____
12. price scale　　　　　　　_____

VI. Complete the following letters with proper words.

Letter 1

March 1, 2016

Dear Sirs,

　　Your company has kindly been introduced to us _____ Messers Freenan & Co. Ltd., Lagos, Nigeria, as prospective buyers of Chinese Cotton Piece Goods. As this _____ falls within the scope of our business activities, we shall be pleased to _____ into direct _____ relations with you at an early _____.

　　To give you a general idea of the various kinds of cotton piece goods now _____ for export, we _____ a brochure and a price list. Quotations and samples will be airmailed to you on _____ of your specific inquiry.

　　We are looking forward _____ your favorable reply.

Yours faithfully,

Letter 2

May 15, 2016

Dear Sirs,

Your name and address were _____ to us by the London Trade Board _____ a large exporter of fabrics of high quality.

We are importers of quality clothing materials, and have large annual _____ from our markets _____ Spain.

We should be obliged if you would _____ us your pattern books showing the complete _____ of these fabrics, _____ with your price list.

We look forward to the pleasure of hearing from you soon.

Yours faithfully,

Letter 3

May 18, 2016

Dear Mr. Jackson,

We were impressed by the _____ of sweaters that were displayed on your stand at the "Menswear Exhibition" that was held in NY last month.

We are a large chain of retailers and are looking for a manufacturer who could _____ us with a wide _____ of sweaters for the teenage market.

If you can _____ orders of over 1,500 garments at one time, please _____ us your current catalogue and price _____. We hope to _____ from you soon.

Yours sincerely,

VII. Translation.

Dear Sirs,

We have learned your name and address in the October issue of *Foreign Trade*. At present, we are interested in your bed-sheets and bath towels.

We take this opportunity to introduce ourselves as one of the largest importers of textiles in the area. We shall appreciate it very much if you will quote us your best CIF C5% London prices, indicating sizes and colors. Meanwhile, please send us some samples and catalogs. If your prices are reasonable and suitable for our market, we shall place a large order with you.

We have been handling textile for over 20 years and have a lot of clients. We would like to know if we could act as your sole agent in this area.

> Your early reply will be highly appreciated.
>
> Yours faithfully,

VIII. Writing.

Letter One

Write to the Overseas Trading Co., Ltd. whose name and address you have learned on the recommendation of the National Bank of Bangladesh. Tell them that you hope to enter into business relations with them. The main line of your business is exporting light industrial products. Samples and catalogues will be sent upon specific inquiries.

Letter Two

Write to Winter & Co., at 164 Royal Parade, Wellington, New Zealand. Acknowledge the receipt of their letter of September 9. Agree to their proposal of establishing relations with you. The bureau concerned in Shanghai will handle the commodity inspection.

Chapter 9

Price Discussion

Lead-in: Case Study

Case One

Jo Wang, sales manager in Excellent Chemical Co., has received an inquiry for PA80000-5AA chemical materials from Mr. Hansson in EVA Technology Co., and is making an offer to the inquiry to facilitate the business.

Case Two

Jeremy Lauwe in Tonton Electronics asks Ms. Anne Wang in Keyway Keyboard Co. who makes an offer to reduce the price of keytops with USA version by 10%, and if accepted intends to purchase 40,000 sets.

Case Three

After the offer and counter-offer, Mr. Jeff in Goodwill Computer Co. disagrees/agrees to the counter-offer from Jerrod in Union Co.

1. Offer

An offer is actually a proposal of certain trade terms and an expression of willingness to make a contract according to the terms proposed. It is made either by a seller, called "selling offer", or by a buyer, called "buying offer" or "bid". In practice, there are two popular types of offers: "firm offer" and "non-firm offer". In the case of firm offer, sellers promise to sell goods at a stated price within a stated period of time and can not take the offer back once it has been accepted. While a non-firm offer has no binding force upon the offerer or offeree and can be taken back at will.

扫描二维码
自学 PPT

When it comes to a firm offer, the information supplied should include name of commodities, quality, quantity and specifications and the details of prices, discounts, terms of payment, packing, insurance, date of delivery, etc. What is more, the period for which the offer is valid must be stated clearly.

(1) Express thanks for the enquiry or acknowledge the receipt of the inquiry.

(2) Give favorable comments on the goods needed if possible.

(3) Supply all the information requested, including name of commodities, quality, quantity and specifications, prices, discounts, terms of payment, packing, insurance, date of delivery, etc.

(4) State clearly the period for which the offer is valid.

(5) Express hope that the offer will be accepted and assure the customer of good service.

Sample 1: Firm Offer

Date: May 23 **To:** Mr. Hansson **From:** Jo Wang **Re:** PA80000-5AA Chemical Material
Dear Mr. Hansson, 　　Thanks for your inquiry of May 21. 　　As requested, we will arrange to send you 2kg of PA80000-5AA chemical materials by EMS post tomorrow for your approval. 　　As to the best price and delivery time, we would like to offer as follows: **FOB price:** $1.16/kg FOB Qingdao by sea **Shipment:** within 20 days after order confirmed **Payment:** by T/T before shipment **Packing:** bulk packing in plastic keg **Validity:** 30 days from the date quoted Please advise your order position soon.   Jo Wang Sales Manager

Sample 2: Non-firm Offer

Date: May 20
To: Mr. Fung
From: Xu Yulin
Re: Your Inquiry for FB Milk Powder

Dear Mr. Fung,

Thank you for your interest in FB Milk Powder. We are happy to make you a special offer, subject to our final confirmation as follows:

The origin is Western Europe, and the quality is "Extra Grade" specifications as per the fax.

Packing: 4 layers paper bags with approx. 17/18 MT per 20' container

Price: $2,000/MT CIF Lumpur

In case you have any further questions, please do not hesitate to contact me.

Sincerely yours,

Xu Yulin
Overseas Sales Department

2. Counter-offer

In a deal, on one hand, the seller with favorable or unfavorable profit will always claim that the profit is minimum, zero or even under the cost, and the buyer, on the other hand, will tend to lower the price as much as possible. Besides, the buyer is also likely to ask for a more favorable payment term, a shorter delivery time or a free-give. Generally speaking, if an offeree partly agrees to or totally disagrees with the offer but puts forward the new suggestion, a "counter-offer" comes into being, which is actually a new offer from the original offer.

When making a counter-offer, the buyer should express regret at inability to accept and state reasons, put forward amendments or new proposals, or suggest that there may be other opportunities to do business together.

(1) Express the thanks for the offer or acknowledge the receipt of the offer.

(2) State the regret that the offer is on the high side or higher than that of the other suppliers.

(3) Give reasons to make such a counter-offer, such as the slow market, severe market competition, a volume order or a limited budget, or directly put forward the target price or terms.

(4) Require the seller to reconsider the offer and provide a better term.

Sample 1: Counter-offer

Date: June 23
To: Ms. Anne Wang
From: Jeremy Lauwe
Re: Keytops with USA Version

Dear Anne,

Thanks for your offer on June 21 for the keytops with USA version.

We find your price is 10% higher. Could you requote us a lower price as we are interested in buying 40,000 sets of keytops.

We are awaiting your answer by return.

Yours,
Jeremy Lauwe

Sample 2: Counter-offer

Date: June 3
To: Xu Yulin
From: Mr. Karl
Re: Your Offer for Men's Shirts

Dear Miss Xu,

We acknowledge receipt of both your offer of May and the samples of men's shirts, and thank you for these.

While appreciating the good quality of your shirts, we find your price is rather too high for the market we wish to supply.

We have also to point out that the men's shirt are available in our market from several European manufacturers, all of them are at prices from 15% to 20% below yours.

Such being the case, we have to ask you to consider if you can reduce your price, say 10%. As our order would be worth around $50,000, you may think it worthwhile to make a concession.

We await with keen interest your immediate reply.

Yours faithfully,
Karl Black

Karl Black
Import Department

3. Acceptance and Refusal

After receiving the counter-offer from the buyer, the seller needs to make a reply of acceptance or refusal, which is usually the case in the trade.

In the case of acceptance, remember that harshness makes no perfect. Regardless of sufficient or insufficient profit margin, the seller will state that there is no profit margin or even under the cost and that the reason to accept is to intend to enter into business relationship with the client or maintain the relation with the regular customer, which facilitates the transactions.

In the case of refusal, the seller should: express the regret to know that the buyer is unsatisfied with offer; state that the offer is the best term almost with zero profit margin; give the reasons to make the refusal, such as good quality, costly materials, increased labor cost, appreciation or the fluctuation of the exchange rate; apologize for the refusal and express the hope for the next cooperation.

There are other cases in the seller's reply to the counter-offer besides the acceptance and refusal. For example, the seller may agree with counter-offer with some additional terms such as "to increase the quantity, change the terms of payment, deliver the goods in one lot instead of several lots, or replace the goods with the alternative"; sometimes the seller may also agree to reduce the price by half as the compromise. In both cases, another counter-offer comes into being.

Sample 1: Acceptance

From: Clark Leony **To:** Tom **Subject:** Your Counter-offer for Backpack
Dear Tom, 　　We've received your counter-offer, which actually leaves us almost no profit at the moment. 　　Considering that you are one of our regular customers and a large volume of 5,000 pieces, we are going to accept your price of \$9/piece CIF Basrah. 　　Please send the order as soon as possible for us to arrange the production. 　　　　　　　　　　　　　　　　　　　　　　　Yours sincerely, 　　　　　　　　　　　　　　　　　　　　　　　Clark Leony

Sample 2: Refusal

Date: June 15
To: Xu Yulin
From: Mr.Karl
Re: Your Counter-offer for Computer Case

We regret to hear that you can not accept the price we offered.

After we carefully checked your target price, we are really sorry to tell you that $18/set is under our cost. To avoid the quality problem after shipment, we are not able to adopt any other alternative for the computer.

Sorry for our inability to help you in this case. However, we hope that we can cooperate with you in the future deals.

Yours sincerely,
Karl
Export Department

Sample 3: Acceptance with Some Terms

To: Paul Lockwood
From: Francesco Marani
Date: July 17
Re: Real Brand Camera No. 900T

Your counter-offer for Real Brand Camera No. 900T has reached us this morning.

After careful consideration we would be willing to accept your price offered. However, in order to speed up the production with more cash flow, we would like to have payment by T/T instead of D/P.

Furthermore, the goods will be dispatched in one lot instead of several lots during a month, which actually saves both of us time and money.

If it is acceptable, please inform us as soon as possible.

Yours sincerely,
Francesco Marani

4. Supplementary Information
1) Incoterms

Incoterms (international commercial terms), developed by ICC in Paris, has been periodically revised to account for changing modes of transport and document delivery. The current versions include Incoterms 2000 and Incoterms 2010. Incoterms 2000 is grouped into 4 categories (Table 9-1).

Table 9-1　Incoterms 2000

Group E	EXW	EX works
Group F	FCA FAS FOB	Free carrier Free alongside ship Free on board
Group C	CFR CIF CPT CIP	Cost and freight Cost, insurance and freight Carriage paid to Carriage and insurance paid to
Group D	DAF DES DEQ DDU DDP	Delivered at frontier Delivered ex ship Delivered ex quay Delivered duty unpaid Delivered duty paid

Incoterms 2010 rules define the responsibilities of buyers and sellers for the delivery of goods under sales contracts. Incoterms 2010 takes into account the latest developments in commercial practice, and updates and consolidates some of the former rules.

A new classification system divides Incoterms 2010 rules into two distinct groups.

(1) Rules for any mode of transport: EXW, FCA, CPT, CIP, DAT, DAP, DDP.

(2) Rules for waterway transport: FAS, FOB, CFR, CIF.

In addition, Incoterms 2010 includes the following contents.

(1) Extensive guidance notes and illustrative graphics to help users efficiently choose the right rule for each transaction.

(2) New classification to help choosing the most suitable rule in relation to the mode of transport.

(3) Advice for the use of electronic procedures.

(4) Information on security-related clearances for shipments.

(5) Advice for the use of Incoterms 2010 in domestic trade.

Besides, it has the following changes.

(1) DAF, DES, DEQ, DDU were deleted.

(2) DAT (delivered at terminal), DAP (delivered at place) have been added.

2) Expressions of Trade Terms

Trade terms are expressed in the unit price of goods. The expression of trade terms is illustrated as follows.

In FOB Shanghai, FOB is the short form for "free on board", Shanghai is the port of shipment. However, if it is expressed as CIF Shanghai, Shanghai turns to be the port of destination.

It is popular to find unit price with commission, such as FOB C2.5% Shanghai, C is "commission", which refers to the money paid by the buyer to salesmen or agents. It is usually a percentage of the money received from the sales made.

The price term of a sales contract involves unit price and total price. Unit price includes the measuring unit, price, money of account and trade terms. For instance, a price term can be worded like this, "$1,500 per m/t CIF London including 3% commission" or "$1,500 per m/t CIF C3% London". The measuring unit includes 6 categories, which are weight (g—gram, kg—kilogram, oz—ounce, lb.—pound, M/T—metric ton); unit (pc—piece, pr—pair, doz—dozen, gr—gross, ctn—carton, pkg—package); length (m—metre, ft—foot, yd—yard); square (sq.m, sq.ft, sq.yd); cubic (cu.m, cu.ft, cu. yd); volume (l—litre, gal—gallon, bu—bushel).

Discount/allowance, provided by the seller to the buyer, is the deduction in the money paid to the seller, and used as an encouragement to the buyer for various purposes. It is also indicated in a price term, for example, "$300 per m/t FOB Shanghai including 2% discount" or "$300 per m/t FOB Shanghai less 2% discount".

3) Subject to Our Final Confirmation

This is a phrase used in a non-firm offer which indicates no definite validity period.

Similar phrases are as follows.

(1) Offer is subject to change without notice.

(2) Offer is subject to goods being unsold.

(3) Offer is subject to prior sale.

While a firm offer is usually with a valid period, phrases commonly used are as follows.

(1) Offer is valid for 5 days.

(2) Subject to your confirmation reaching here on or before the 25th this month.

(3) Subject to your acceptance before the end of this month.

(4) Subject to your reply reaching here by August 15, Beijing time.

(5) Subject to your reply reaching here within 5 days.

4) MT

MT is the short form of "metric ton".

1 metric ton = 2,204.6 lb = 1,000 kg (metric system)

1 short ton = 2,000 lb = 0.907 MT (US System)

1 long ton = 2,240 lb = 1.016 MT (British System)

5. Useful Expressions

(1) *We thank you for your enquiry of Feb. 2 and are pleased to inform you we are in good connections with the best manufacturers in the country.*

(2) *Thank you for your letter of January 14.*

(3) *We have much pleasure in enclosing a quotation sheet for our products and*

trust that their high quality will induce you to place a trial order.

(4) *In accordance with the request of ... at the Guangzhou Fair, we have pleasure in sending you herewith the samples and a price list for ...*

(5) *We take pleasure in making you an offer as required by you, subject to our final confirmation.*

(6) *We are glad to learn from your enquiry of February 8 that you are interested in our ladies' blouses. As requested our catalogue and price list are enclosed together with details of our sale conditions.*

(7) *We were pleased to receive your enquiry of March 10 for our Portable Mixer Model PM-222.*

(8) *We are pleased to quote you the best price.*

(9) *We can supply most items from stock and will have no trouble in meeting your delivery.*

(10) *We can allow you a special discount of 2% on the prices quoted for a quantity of 50 or more.*

(11) *We would like to draw your attention to the trade and quantity discount we are offering in our publicity brochure, which may be of particular interest to you.*

(12) *We regret that it is impossible to accept your counter-offer, even to meet you half way; the price of raw material has advanced 20% and we shall shortly be issuing an advanced price list.*

(13) *Although we are anxious to open up business with you, we regret that it is impossible for us to allow the reduction asked for, because we have already cut our prices to the lowest point after examining our cost calculations.*

(14) *It would be greatly to your interest to make a trial of these goods.*

(15) *May we expect a trial order from you while prices are greatly in your favor?*

(16) *As there is a heavy demand at this time of the year for heaters, you will have to allow at least 6 weeks for delivery.*

(17) *We do not see any advantage in your quotations, and would like to know whether you have any better value to offer.*

(18) *We desire to call your attention to our special offer. You will readily understand that this offer is good only for acceptance reaching us before the end of ... In view of the heavy demand for this line, we advise you to send orders as soon as possible.*

(19) *Your competitors are offering considerably lower prices and unless you can reduce your quotations we shall have to buy elsewhere.*

(20) *We thank you for your offer, but we are buying at lower prices. Are these best prices you can offer?*

Exercises

I. Choose the appropriate word or words to complete the sentences.

1. We (offer, quote) you for 500 sets of sewing machines (at, on) $50 (on, at, of) CIF Lagos basis (for, in) June/July shipment.
2. There is (not, no) possibility (of doing, to do) business at this price.
3. We confirm (having sent, sending, to send) you a cable this morning, as per (confirmation copy, duplicate copy, carbon copy) enclosed.
4. Should you (prepared, be prepared) to (reduce, down) the price by 5%, we (will, would, shall) place our trial order (on, upon, with) you.
5. We write you today (on, in) the hope of entering into (business, business relations, business relation) with you.
6. We shall (try, make) our best to (fit, satisfy) your (requirement, requirements).
7. We need all the (necessary, needful) (informations, information) regarding your products (exporting, exported, exportable) now.
8. We (often, always) (adhere, adhere to) the (principle, basis) of equality and mutual benefit (with, in, on) our trade (with, in, of) foreign countries.

II. Arrange the following words and phrases in their proper order.

1. you will agree that   the most selective buyers
   when you see our samples   will appeal to
   and the high standard of craftsmanship   we think that
   the quality of the material used

   _____

   _____

   _____

2. to meet your requirement   once our supplies are replenished
   we are at present unable   for the captioned articles
   though   we shall be only too pleased
   to revert to the matter

   _____

   _____

   _____

Chapter 9 Price Discussion

3. and look forward to your first order   we should like to
   details of which   such as stainless steel kitchenware
   you will find in the catalogue   our other products
   draw your attention to

   _____
   _____
   _____

4. steel tapes   CFR Lagos
   at your request   for 1,000 dozen
   we are now offering you   at $5 per dz

   _____
   _____
   _____

5. at considerably lower prices   represent better value
   and therefore   our competitors
   are obviously superior in quality   we are well aware that
   but our products   are quoting

   _____
   _____
   _____

III. Fill in the blanks.

   1. As the market is _____ your price is _____ on the _____ side.
   2. We _____ from your letter of March 20, that you are _____ the _____ for black tea.
   3. We cannot _____ _____ _____ clear to reduce the price to the level you _____.
   4. We hope to _____ business at something _____ our level.
   5. You _____ _____ assured that the goods under Contract No. 4546 will be shipped _____ _____.
   6. Since your price is _____ _____ _____ with the prevailing market, it is not _____ for the market at our _____.
   7. While we appreciate your intention, we regret that we _____ entertain any fresh orders.
   8. As soon as we are _____ a _____ to make an _____ for walnuts, we shall _____ you telegraphically.
   9. We are enclosing a _____ of our new products for your _____.

10. We take _____ in informing you that we are _____ a _____ to accept new orders.

11. We have cut our price to the limit. We regret, therefore, being unable to comply _____ your request for further reduction.

12. As business has been done extensively _____ your market _____ this price, we regret that we can not accept your counter-offer. It is our hope that you would reconsider the matter and let us know _____ return.

IV. Translation.

Dear Mary,

Thank you for the information of the business card holder. I have not yet had a decision from the client. They have a number of layers of people to go through for final decisions. As soon as I have any information, I will advise you. I expect the decision will be made this week or as late as next week. I apologize for any inconvenience.

Kind regards,
Rose

琼斯先生：

感谢贵公司 8 月 1 日寄来的询价单，该函及所附的样品均已收悉。

鉴于该样品检验的结果，我们向贵公司保证，敝公司能够制造与该样品相同型号与品质的产品。

基于贵公司每年 10 万双的需求量，我方报盘如下。

价格：CIF 大连每双 25 美元。

包装：塑料袋，外包装为纸板箱。

支付：即期的、不可撤销的、保兑的信用证。

交货：收到订单后的 90 天内，即 11 月、12 月船期。

有效期：8 月 31 日。

我们可向贵公司保证，此价格是基于上述数量的最低价。其他技术性事项可参阅我公司的商品手册。

如有其他问题，请多多指点。

谨致问候
李平

附件：商品手册一本

V. Give the English or Chinese equivalents of the followings.

1. 秋季目录　　　　＿＿＿＿＿＿＿＿＿＿＿＿＿＿
2. 皮重　　　　　　＿＿＿＿＿＿＿＿＿＿＿＿＿＿
3. 即期汇票　　　　＿＿＿＿＿＿＿＿＿＿＿＿＿＿
4. 实盘　　　　　　＿＿＿＿＿＿＿＿＿＿＿＿＿＿
5. 美式键盘　　　　＿＿＿＿＿＿＿＿＿＿＿＿＿＿
6. T/T　　　　　　＿＿＿＿＿＿＿＿＿＿＿＿＿＿
7. item number　　＿＿＿＿＿＿＿＿＿＿＿＿＿＿
8. computer case　 ＿＿＿＿＿＿＿＿＿＿＿＿＿＿
9. alternative　　　＿＿＿＿＿＿＿＿＿＿＿＿＿＿
10. overseas department　＿＿＿＿＿＿＿＿＿＿＿＿＿＿

VI. Complete the following letters with proper words.

Letter 1

Dear Mike,

Re: Plush Toys

Thank you for your _____ of November 13.

We would like to _____ as follows based on per 20' FCL.

Name of the commodity: KB5411 Bear in Ballet Costume

_____: 12 pcs/ctn, 162cartons/20' FCL

Price: $ 9/pc CIFC3 Amsterdam

Shipment: to be _____ within 2 months from receipt of the relevant L/C

Payment: By sight L/C

Insurance: for 110% of _____ value covering all risks and war risks

We will keep this offer _____ only for 7 days.

　　　　　　　　　　　　　　　　　　　　　　　　　　Yours truly,

Letter 2

Dear Sirs,

Re: Woolen Carpet

Thank you for your letter of October 12, _____ us woolen carpet.

However, we very much regret to state that we find the _____ is too high.

Information indicates that the same _____ made in China sold at much lower price. So if you should reduce your price _____ 3%, we might _____ to terms.

Considering our long-standing business relationship, we make you such a _____.

Hope you take our suggestion into consideration and give us your _____ as soon as possible.

Yours truly,

VII. Writing.

Letter 1

Write a letter to offer "Jade Rabbit" brand radios to the Oriental Trading Co. at £40 per set CIF London, June shipment, commission 3%, and payment by L/C at sight.

Letter 2

Please read the following offer and then make a counter-offer as a buyer.

Dear Troy,

Re: Our Offer for Sweater

Thank you for your fax of December 20 and your interest in our sweater. As requested we would offer as follows:

Price: $35/dozen FOB Taiwan

Delivery: within 30 days after receipt of the L/C

Packing: standard export packing

Payment: by confirmed irrevocable sight L/C

Minimum order: 1,000 dozens

Validity: 30 days

Samples will be posted after the receipt of the charge.

Please don't hesitate to inform us the further information needed.

Yours truly,
Jean Wung

Chapter 10

Order and Reply

Lead-in: Case Study

Huaxin Trading Co., Ltd. and James Brown and Sons have undergone a serial of correspondence and reached an agreement to the following price terms.

Art. No.	Commodity	Unit	Quantity	Unit Price ($)	Amount ($)
	Chinese ceramic dinner-ware				CIFC5 Toronto
HX1115	35 PCS dinnerware and tea set	Set	542	23.5	12,737.00
HX2012	20 PCS dinnerware set	Set	800	20.4	16,320.00
HX4405	47 PCS dinnerware set	Set	443	23.2	10,277.60
HX4510	95 PCS dinnerware set	Set	254	30.1	7,645.40
					46,980.00

However, besides the price there are still some other essential terms to discuss before the signing of contract, such as terms of payment, packing, shipment and insurance. Please continue the correspondence until an order is placed and the contract is signed.

扫描二维码
自学 PPT

An order is a formal request for a certain quantity of specific goods at a certain price to be fulfilled within a certain period of time. An order must keep the important principle of clarity and accuracy so as to avoid misunderstandings and troubles in future. For this reason an order usually includes such details as:

(1) Quality descriptions.
(2) Quantity statement.
(3) All documents required.
(4) Price and the mode of payment.
(5) Packing and marking requirements.
(6) Shipping or forwarding instructions.

(7) Other necessary details.

When placing an order, the writer may express the hope of being given prompt and careful attention to the order besides the details mentioned above.

An order may take the form of a letter, a telegram, a telex message, a fax, or a printed order form. Most ordering is done on standardized order forms, purchase forms, and requisition forms, and is handled by means of standardized procedures.

After the receipt of the order, the seller should lose no time to state the acknowledgment either by a printed acknowledgment form or a letter, or both. The following are what should be done for acknowledgment.

(1) Acknowledge the order with expression of thanks.

(2) Give the seller's reference number.

(3) Restate the contents of the order and where possible add a few favorable comments on the goods ordered.

(4) Restate the shipping instructions, such as the date of shipment and the port of destination.

(5) Restate the terms of payment.

(6) Draw attention to other products likely to be of interest.

(7) Assure the buyer of prompt and careful execution of order and express your desire for future orders and enclose S/C in duplicate for counter-signature.

If turning down an order, the seller should explain the reason, show appreciation of the buyer's confidence in the seller's company and goods, express regret of inability to be helpful and the wish for further contacts, i.e., be polite and generalize the terms so that the buyer does not think the refusal only applies to him.

Sample 1: Initial Order

November 11, 2016
To: Jones Wou
From: Ann
Re: Initial Order No. 101

Dear Mr. Wou,

    Thank you for your letter of November 9. We find both quality and prices satisfactory and would like to place an order with you for the following items on the understanding that they will be supplied from current stock.
Cargo: cotton prints
Unit price: 40 cents/y CIF Liverpool
Quantity: 700 yards
Payment terms: by confirmed irrevocable L/C

Shipment: Dec. shipment
Insurance: all risks

    Please send us your S/C in duplicate.

Ann

Sample 2: Acknowledgment of the Initial Order

November 12, 2016
To: Ann
From: Jones Wou
Re: Your Initial Order No. 101

Dear Ms. Ann,

    Thank you for your order for our cotton prints and welcome you as one of our customers.

    We confirm our acceptance of your order No. 101 and will supply the goods in due course. The S/C has been signed and sent to you under separate cover.

    We are enclosing a copy of our latest catalogue and price list and hope that our handling of this initial order will lead to further business between us and mark the beginning of a happy relationship.

Yours sincerely,
Jones Wou

Sample 3: Order from the Buyer

February 17, 2016
To: Eunice Chang
From: Lester Bemstein

Dear Mr. Chang,

    Thanks for your yesterday's E-mail and the fine price you made us for iPad 5.

    We accept your price and terms and would like to confirm our firm order No. MA-123 as per the copy enclosed.

    Please do 100% test before shipment to make sure the quality and ship the goods on time.

    Please confirm your acceptance by fax and send us a pro forma invoice as soon as possible for opening L/C.

Lester Bemstein

Sample 4: Acknowledgment of the Order

February 18, 2016
To: Lester Bemstein
From: Eunice Chang

Dear Mr. Bemstein,
  Our Ref. P/I 103-B
  Many thanks for your order of February 17 and we confirm the acceptance of your order No. 123. We also confirm that we will do 100% test before shipment and will proceed as stipulated in the order.
  The duly singed P.O. is appended. Enclosed please find our pro forma invoice P/I 103-B as requested for opening L/C.
  We look forward to fostering and strengthening our future business cooperation.

                       Eunice Chang

Sample 5: Reply to Delay the Supply of the Order

February 18, 2016
To: Lester Bemstein
From: Eunice Chang

Dear Mr. Bemstein,
  Many thanks for your order of February 17 but we regret that we are unable to execute the order because of the heavy demand recently.
  We promise to replenish our inventory in 2 months and hope that it will not be inconvenient for you to allow us one month extension.
  We shall be grateful if you could confirm your order on the revised conditions.

                       Eunice Chang

Sample 6: Refusal of the Order

July 25, 2016
To: Mr. Augustatos
From: Helen

  Thank you for your order of July 10 for 300 pairs of children shoes. But we very much regret to say that we are now unable to supply the goods you ordered immediately because of the heavy demand for the goods.
  The manufacturer has promised us a further supply at the end of this year. And we will notify you as soon as possible.

> Meanwhile, we are enclosing a booklet of our other models for your reference. We believe that they will meet your need.
>
> Please contact us if we can be of any help to you.

1. Supplementary Information
1) Pro Forma Invoice

Pro forma invoice is an invoice sent for form's sake and does not bind either the seller or the buyer. A pro forma invoice is not necessarily involved in every transaction. It is generally used to serve as a formal quotation or as a price reference and enable the buyer to make the necessary preliminary arrangements, such as obtaining an import license for the goods he would like to order. Contained in a pro forma invoice are usually the descriptions of the goods, quantity, price, terms of payment, time of shipment, but these do not involve the seller in any contractual obligations. Its contents are to a great extend similar to a commercial one.

2) Commercial Invoice

Commercial invoice is a document prepared by the seller and addressed to the buyer, describing the goods, price and the shipping terms. It serves to provide the complete information on a transaction between the buyer and the seller. Its primary function is to indicate to the buyer the sale of goods at its price terms on the part of the seller and to check the price and the goods bought on the part of the buyer. It's usually made out in triplicate or quadruplicate. The commercial invoice generally bears the seller's own heading in its top. It contains the following information.

(1) Invoice or commercial invoice.

(2) Name and address of the buyer and the seller and the date of invoice.

(3) Complete description of the goods and its packing. If the payment is to be effected by means of a documentary credit, this description must exactly conform to that given in the credit.

(4) Unit price and price terms.

(5) Terms of settlement such as by documentary L/C. In the case of settlement by L/C, the name of the issuing bank and L/C number should be shown thereon.

(6) Shipping marks and numbers, weight and/or quantity of goods, and the name of the vessel if known.

(7) Seller's signature.

(8) Port of loading and discharge or place of receipt and delivery.

(9) Number of the contract and the invoice.

It should be reiterated that all invoices must be correct, include all details required by the buyer, and conform to those regulations governing import licenses, customs duties and exchange controls in the buyer's country.

3) Other Invoices

Other invoices include customs invoice, shipping invoice, sample invoice, consular invoice, and visaed invoice.

4) Order

Order from the buyer usually carries the name as purchase order, order sheet, indent, purchase contract, purchase agreement, purchase confirmation, purchase note. Different types of the order are trial order, sample order, initial order, small order, formal order, large order (big order), repeat order, minimum order, regular order.

2. Useful Expression

(1) *We are pleased to place the following orders with you if you can guarantee shipment from Shanghai to Singapore by October 9.*

(2) *We shall place a large order with you provided the quantity of the goods and shipping period meet our requirements.*

(3) *If this first order is satisfactorily executed, we shall place further orders with you.*

(4) *The material supplied must be absolutely waterproof, and we place our order subject to this guarantee.*

(5) *We are pleased to find that your materials appear to be of fine quality. As a trial, we are delighted to send you a small order for 2,500 dozen rubber shoes.*

(6) *We have the pleasure of sending you an order for 1,000 dozen umbrellas, at $45 per dozen CIF New York, based on your catalog No. 51 of July 1. We trust the prices mentioned therein are still in force.*

(7) *We order 100 units of Italian furniture No. TS11 at $300 per unit FOB Genoa. If this order is acceptable, please let us know by SWIFT.*

(8) *We enclosed a trial order. If the quality is up to our expectation, we shall send further orders in the near future. Your prompt attention to this order will be appreciated.*

(9) *We are pleased to enclose an order we have received from Messrs Grayson Bros for 300 dozen pairs of "Moonlight" rubber shoes.*

(10) *We enclosed our order, but must point out that the falling market here will leave us little or no margin of profit. We must ask you for a better price in respect of future supplies.*

(11) *Your samples of tea have received favorable reaction from our clients, and we are pleased to enclose our order for 400 cartons.*

(12) *We are pleased to place you an order for 100,000 sets of MP3 players.*

(13) *We are sorry to ask you to reduce 1,000 pcs from order No.416 due to economic depression.*

(14) *We cannot accept your quantity increase because we have completed*

the production and it is difficult to prepare the material for the increased small quantity.

I. **Correct inappropriate words and expressions.**

1. Please send us as soon as possible the following goods, which listed in your current spring catalogue.
2. The enclosed order is given strictly on the condition which shipment must be made not later than the first day of May.
3. We reserve the right to cancel this order except the goods are in our hands at the end of June.
4. We are handling your order with great care and you can depend on us effecting delivery well within your time limit.
5. You may rest assured that fresh supplies are due to arriving early next month.
6. If the quality of your goods is satisfied, we will place a large order with you.
7. Very much we would like to supply you the product, we are unable to fill your order owing to the heavy backlog of commitments.
8. We cannot make you an offer, as the goods are not in stock.

II. **Fill in the blanks.**

1. Our offer is _____ subject to your _____ _____ one week.
2. We have established _____ irrevocable letter of credit _____ the Bank of China, Shanghai.
3. Please keep us _____ _____ the response to our new product in your market.
4. Please _____ one copy of purchase confirmation completed _____ your counter-signature.
5. We confirm telegrams exchanged resulting _____ the sale to you of 100 tons grounding.
6. We are sending you our sales contract No. 175 _____ duplicate.
7. We expect to put _____ the deal.
8. We trust that you will give special care to the goods, _____ they _____ be damaged.
9. Your price was rather _____ the high side, so we are afraid we can not _____ your offer.

10. You will be advised _____ time when the machines are ready _____ shipment.

11. The relative L/C will be airmailed soon and you are requested to ship the above lot _____ the first available steamer upon receipt _____ our L/C.

12. We have pleasure _____ sending you the attached orders confirmation No. 350, _____ our recent purchase _____ you of 1,500 cowhides.

III. **Give the English or Chinese equivalents of the followings.**

1. 确认订单 _____
2. 下订单 _____
3. 取消订单 _____
4. 续订 _____
5. 库存 _____
6. to adjust the price _____
7. to hold to the contract _____
8. discrepancy _____
9. current stock _____
10. trial order _____

IV. **Arrange the following words and phrases in their proper order.**

1. at the named prices   to give you an order
   they will be supplied   for the following items
   we are pleased   on the understanding that
   from current stock

   _____
   _____

2. and please sign and return   for the order No. GD34
   to us   in duplicate
   thank you very much
   for our file   to enclose
   one copy of which   our sales confirmation No. 9975
   we are pleased

   _____
   _____
   _____

3. our immediate attention   is receiving
   within your time limit   and
   your order   can be delivered well

   _____
   _____

4. by 5%   while
   in the prices of raw materials   we have to explain that
   thank you for your order   owing to a corresponding rise
   our price has increased

   _____
   _____

5. we are ready   in order to finalize
   a 5% discount   the first transaction between us
   to allow you   the quantity to 1,000
   if you can increase   however

   _____
   _____
   _____

V. Translation.

Passage 1

接到你公司 9 月 5 日印花细布（printing shirting）订单，非常高兴，并欢迎你公司成为我公司的客户之一。

确认按你方来信列明价格供应印花细布，并已安排下周由"公主号"轮装出。

深信你公司收到货物后，定会感到完全满意。你公司也许不甚知道我公司的经营范围，现附上目录一份。希望这首批订单将带来彼此更多的业务往来，展开愉快的工作关系。

Passage 2

Re: O/No. 16620 Resistors

We have found that we are overstocked on some items. Please advise if you will accept the following reductions/cancellations:

Zero ohm 1/4W

> 120 ohm 1/4W
>
> Please review and advise by return.
>
> If you cannot accept to cancel the quantity listed above, could you accept a partial reduction?
>
> Please advise.

VI. Complete the following letters with proper words.

Letter 1

> Dear Sirs,
>
> We thank you _____ your quotation of the 13th April and for the _____ tin so kindly sent us.
>
> As your _____ are quite up to our expectations, we are pleased to _____ our order form of the "Rainbow" tea. You will observe that delivery is to be _____ by the 19th April.
>
> We have every reason to believe that this _____ will be successful, and we hope to entrust you with further _____ in the near future.
>
> Yours faithfully,
> Smith & Sons

Letter 2

> Dear Mr. Augustatos,
>
> We received your order, in which you _____ us the quantity of 2 containers only.
>
> As _____ in our last correspondence, we would give you 1.5% discount only on the _____ of the order for total 3 containers. So, please reconfirm if you want to _____ the quantity to 3 containers to get the 1.5% discount, or only order 2 containers _____ any discount.
>
> We are looking forward to receiving your order soon.

Letter 3

> Dear Sirs,
>
> We have _____ the _____ shipment ex S.S. "Blue Seas" and are _____ to inform you that we _____ the goods quite _____.
>
> _____ we believe we can sell additional _____ in this market, we wish to place with you a _____ order for 500 dozens of the _____ style and sizes.
>
> We would be _____ if you could _____ early shipment of this repeat order as we are in _____ need of the goods.

If the goods are not available from _____, we would be grateful if you could _____ us, with full particulars of the replacement goods which can be shipped from stock.

Yours faithfully,

Letter 4

Dear Ms. Green,

    We are pleased to _____ your letter of 14th March in _____ us that you are satisfied with our ladies' tights _____ to you per S.S. "Blue Seas". We also _____ that you wish to _____ a repeat order.

    We _____ that we cannot at present _____ any new orders for Baletto ladies' tights _____ to heavy orders.

    We are, however, _____ your order before us. As soon as we are in a _____ to accept new orders, we will _____ you by E-mail.

    With _____ to stock lines, we _____ a list for your _____. Should you be _____ in any of these, please let us know your _____, stating _____, style and _____.

Chapter 11

Payment

> **Lead-in: Case Study**
>
> **Case 1**
>
> Wolf International trading Co., Ltd. has sent the order No. DSG267 covering enamelware in the amount of $9,980 to you. They would like to pay by D/P after sight. Would you agree? Write a letter to elaborate your ideas on terms of payment.
>
> **Case 2**
>
> Cotton Weavers Ltd., has purchased 3,000 pieces of cotton print for delivery in December. As the goods have been ready for shipment for a long time, write a letter to the buyer urging him to establish the covering L/C immediately.

扫描二维码
自学 PPT

Payment plays a vital role in the international trade, which, if not ensured, will result in total failure of the transaction. There are several commonly used terms of payment nowadays: remittance, L/C, collection, open account, installment, on consignment, cash on delivery and cash with order.

In the first deal mostly both sides would prefer L/C because of its safety, but due to its expensive bank charges and a financial burden on the buyer resulting from the tie-up fund for over 30 days, in usual practice only when the deal is over $5,000 L/C will be applied. Letters regarding payment by L/C often fall into the following types: informing the open of L/C, urging establishment of L/C, amending L/C or asking for extension of L/C.

To inform the opening of the L/C, you should: inform the seller the effect of the payment, including the terms of payment, total amount, and the quantity of the goods; ask for the confirmation of the shipment.

Messages urging establishment of L/C must be written with tact. The first message sent should be a polite note, which says that the goods are ready but the relevant L/C has not yet come to hand. It is usually composed by: informing the buyer the goods are ready for shipment; emphasizing the closing date for shipment; urging the establishment of the L/C; giving a motivating ending.

When the seller receives the relevant L/C, he/she should make a thorough check to see whether the clauses stated in the L/C are in full compliance with terms in the sales contract. If any discrepancies are found, the seller should send an advice to the buyer, asking him/her to amend them. Not just the seller can ask for amendment to the L/C, the buyer can also ask for amendment if he/she finds something in the L/C needs to be altered. But the buyer needs to obtain consent from the seller and instruct the opening bank to amend the L/C. The basic writing structure to ask for amendment goes as follows.

(1) To identify the reference.
(2) To state the problem and give the reason for questing for amendment.
(3) To make a suggestion.
(4) To urge a prompt reply.

When it comes to the deal between the regular customer, payment terms will vary a lot based on the usual practice.

Sample 1: Proposal for Payment by L/C from the Seller

CHINA NATIONAL IMPORT AND EXPORT CORPORATION

February 17, 2016
To: Mr. Woo < Messrs Aullivan & Son@gmail.com>
From: Tang Wanliang <CNIEC@qq.com>
Re: Payment by L/C

Dear Mr. Woo,

Thanks for your order No. 3325 and wish to say that we have adequate stocks of Type EM 127DN tapes in our warehouse, and the delivery date can be met.

Payment by irrevocable letter of credit is convenient for us, and we shall draw a 60 days bill on your bank.

We are now waiting for the arrival of your L/C, on receipt of which we shall make the necessary arrangements for the shipment of your order. Any request for further assistance or information will receive our immediate attention.

Sincerely yours,
Tang Wanliang
Overseas Sales Director

扫描二维码
浏览视频
"Trade Finance in the Spotlight—Letters of Credit"

Sample 2: Proposal for Payment by L/C from the Buyer

October 27, 2016
To: Leon<Irina Office Equipment Co.Ltd.@hotmail. com>
From: Hamzza<Niger Trading@google.com>
Re: L/C Payment

Dear Leon,

We would like to place an order for 500 microphones at your price of $50 each CIF Logos, for shipment during November/December.

We would like to pay for this order by a 30 days L/C. This is an order involving $25,000 and since we have only moderate cash reserves, tying up funds for 1 or 2 months would be inconvenient for us.

We much appreciate the support you have given us in the past and would be most grateful if you could extend this favor to us. If you agree to the terms, please send us your contract. On receipt, we will establish the relevant L/C immediately.

Yours faithfully,
Hamzza

Sample 3: Asking to Ship an Order Cash on Delivery

Huangshan Tea Exporting Co., Ltd.

June 6, 2016
To: Mr. Augustatos
From: Geng Shuying
Re: Cash on Delivery

Dear Mr. Augustatos,

Thank you for your order No. 5656 of 30 May for 500 cases of black tea.

We would like to arrange immediate shipment. Unfortunately, we do not have sufficient credit information to offer you open account terms at this time.

Would it be acceptable to ship this order cash on delivery?

If you wish to receive open account terms for your next order, please provide us with the standard financial statement and bank reference. This information will be held in strict confidence.

We look forward to hearing from you.

Yours sincerely,
Geng Shuying
Export Manager

Sample 4: Informing the Establishment of L/C

Burgeon International Trading Co., Ltd.
March 1, 2016 **To:** Mike **From:** Bill D. H.
Dear Mike, 　　We are pleased to let you know that we have instructed Federal Commercial Bank, Shanghai Branch to open an irrevocable letter of credit for $1,010,000 in your favor. This should cover CIF shipment and bank charges, and the credit is valid until July 15, 2016. 　　You will receive confirmation from our bank's correspondent, Federal Commercial Bank, Los Angeles and you may draw on them at 60 days for the amount of the L/C. When submitting your draft, would you please enclose the following documents? 　　Bill of Lading (6 copies) 　　Invoice CIF Shanghai (4 copies) 　　A.R. Insurance Policy for $1,111,000 　　Please advise us as soon as you have arranged the shipment. 　　　　　　　　　　　　　　　　　　　　　　　　　　Sincerely, 　　　　　　　　　　　　　　　　　　　　　　　　　　Bill D. H. 　　　　　　　　　　　　　　　　　　　　　　　　　　Manager 　　　　　　　　　　　　　　　　　　　　　　　　　　Import Department

Sample 5: Urging the Establishment of L/C

GENTPACE INTERNATIONAL TRADING CO., LTD.
May 5, 2016 **To:** Mr. Amin **ATT:** General Manager **From:** Wang Ju
Dear Mr. Amin, 　　We refer to your order for 500 dozen pairs of jeans and our sales confirmation No. 225. 　　We would like to remind you that the delivery date is approaching and we have not yet received the covering letter of credit. 　　We would be grateful if you would expedite the establishment of the L/C so that we can ship the order on time.

In order to avoid any further delay, please make sure that the L/C instructions are in accordance with the terms of the contract.

We look forward to receiving your response at an early date.

Sincerely yours,
Wang Ju

Sample 6: Amending L/C

June 15, 2016
To: Mr. Boosh
ATT: Financial Department
From: Picker
Re: L/C 800918 for Shipment

Dear Mr. Boosh,

We regret to inform you that we can only ship goods at the end of June if we can receive your following amendments by SWIFT before this week.

(1) Please change the price term to CIF Shanghai, China.

(2) Transshipment is to be allowed.

(3) Extend the latest shipping date to July 25, 2016 and the validity of the L/C to August 10, 2016.

We will proceed the packing and inspection only upon receipt of your above amendments. To show our sincerity, we will pay for the amendment charge and will return you the freight cost from Shanghai to HK after shipment is made.

Please move faster on this amendment to avoid the delay in shipment. Please understand that our bank can only make the payment to us upon receipt of your correction.

We are really sorry for the trouble caused and appreciate your great help on the matter.

Yours sincerely,
Picker
General Manager

1. Supplementary Information
1) Remittance

Remittance includes telegraphic transfer (T/T), mail transfer (M/T). The simple expression of "Payment by T/T" will lead to dispute. Usually it should be stated as "Payment: by T/T before shipment" or "Payment: by T/T within 30 days after shipment".

2) Cash with Order

Cash with order requires the buyer place the funds at the disposal of the seller prior to shipment of the goods or provision of services. It is used when the buyer's credit is doubtful, when there is an unstable political or economic environment in the buyer's country, and/or if there is a potential delay in the receipt of funds from the buyer, perhaps due to events beyond control. Advantage to the seller is immediate use of funds. Disadvantages to the buyer are that he pays in advance tying up his capital prior to receipt of the goods or services, that he has no assurance that what he has contracted for will be supplied, received in a timely fashion, and received in the quality or quantity ordered.

3) Open Account

Open account is used in the long-term purchase or several transactions per month. Usually the exporter delivers the goods first and then the importer pays to the exporter. We can have mail transfer (M/T), telegraphic transfer (T/T), and demand draft (D/D) in such payment term.

4) Collection

Collection is an arrangement whereby the goods are shipped and the relevant bill of exchange is drawn by the seller on the buyer, and/or document(s) is sent to the seller's bank with clear instructions for collection through one of its correspondent banks located in the domicile of the buyer. Collection is of two types: collection on clean bill of exchange and collection on bill of exchange with document (or called documentary collection). The later can also be divided into D/P (D/P at sight and D/P at XX days after sight) and D/A. Collection on clean bill of exchange is seldom used in foreign trade except a balance of payment or some extra charges involved in the trade are to be collected.

2. Useful Expression

(1) *D/P is applicable only if the amount involved for each transaction is less than $1,000.*

(2) *Please expedite the L/C so that we may execute the order smoothly.*

(3) *The shipment date is approaching. It would be advisable for you to open the L/C covering your order No. 751 as early as possible so as to enable us to effect shipment within the stipulated time limit.*

(4) *Please see to it that payment is made by confirmed, irrevocable L/C in our favor, available by draft at sight, and allowing transshipment and partial shipment.*

(5) *We have instructed the Bank of Toronto to open L/C for $20,000/order No. 25/1,000 casks of iron nails in your favor.*

(6) *We have instructed the Standard Chartered Bank, Hong Kong to telegraph the sum of $20,000 for the credit of your account at the BOC, Shanghai.*

扫描二维码
浏览视频
"Overview of International Payment Method"

(7) We have extended the shipment and validity dates of the L/C to October 15 and 31 respectively.

(8) The buyer shall pay the total value to the seller in advance by T/T not later than May 15.

(9) It has been our usual practice to do business with payment by D/P at sight instead of by L/C. we should, therefore, like you to accept D/P terms for this transaction and future ones.

(10) Your proposal for payment by time draft for Order No. 1156 is acceptable to us, and we shall draw on you at 60 days' sight after the goods have been shipped. Please honor our draft when it falls due.

(11) In order to pave the way for your pushing the sale of our products in your market, we will accept payment by D/P at sight as a special accommodation.

(12) Your request for payment by D/P has been taken into consideration. In view of the small amount of this transaction, we are prepared to effect shipment on this basis.

(13) In accordance with the terms of contract No.567, we prepare to open the covering L/C within this week, and shall advise you by cable as soon as it is opened. We expect your best cooperation in the execution of this order.

(14) Just a line to inform you that we have today opened an L/C to cover our purchase of surgical instruments.

(15) We have instructed our bank to issue a confirmed, irrevocable L/C in your favor.

(16) As soon as I hear from you that the goods are ready for shipment, I shall ask the buyer to establish an L/C.

(17) Our usual mode of payment is by confirmed, irrevocable L/C, available by draft at sight for the full amount of the invoice value to be established in our favor through a bank acceptable to us.

(18) In order to cover this order we have established an irrevocable and confirmed L/C in your favor through Barclays Bank, London.

(19) We have opened an irrevocable L/C No. GB418 through the Citi Bank, NY.

Exercises

I. Choose the appropriate word or words to complete the sentences.

1. Mr. Smith will make a note (of, for, to, against) Mr. Sanchez's request for consular invoice.
2. Payments should be made (at, upon, by, after) sight draft.
3. Payment by L/C is our method of (negotiating, settling, financing, assisting)

trade in chemicals.
4. If D/A is possible, it will help ease the (license, licensing, to license, licensed) problem.
5. Mr. Yin could agree (with, to, in, over) D/P terms.
6. 90% of the credit amount must be paid (at, by, against, when) the presentation of documents.
7. You don't say whether you wish the transaction to be (at, by, on, in) cash or (at, by, on, in) credit.
8. We have opened an L/C in your favor (at, by, on, in) the amount of HKD20,000.
9. The deal will be done on the basis that payment is made (with, to, in, over) advance, (at, by, on, in) installment (on, of, for, to) delivery.
10. The check will soon fall (due, short, out, in).

II. **Fill in the blanks.**

1. As usual, for the value of the goods we are _____ on you at 60 days in favor of the Bank of China and trust you will _____ our draft upon _____.
2. We regret to learn from our bankers that you refuse to _____ our draft without giving any reasons.
3. We are drawing _____ you at sight and sending the documents _____ the Bank of China for _____.
4. _____ is made in your letter of December 15 and ours of November 30.
5. We consider it _____ to make it _____ in the first place.
6. We hope that this trial shipment will _____ to your entire satisfaction and will lead to _____.
7. It appears that the stipulations in the L/C are not _____ agreement _____ the contract.
8. Please advise us whether your buyers approve _____ the design.
9. We are agreeable _____ your suggestion.
10. We shall _____ delivery of the goods as soon as they are released from the customs.

III. **Give the English or Chinese equivalents of the followings.**

1. 开立信用证　　_____
2. 信用证指示　　_____
3. 托收　　　　　_____
4. 货到付款　　　_____

5. 预付货款 _____
6. 赊销 _____
7. D/P _____
8. sight draft _____
9. installment _____
10. down payment _____
11. cash reserves _____
12. to extend the L/C _____

IV. Arrange the following words and phrases in their proper order.

1. at 60 days' sight   with regard to terms of payment
   being unable   for D/A
   to consider your request   we regret

   _____
   _____

2. what difficulties   upon receipt of this letter
   in opening the L/C   you actually have
   please let us know

   _____
   _____

3. during this sales-pushing stage   we are pleased
   to accept   as a special accommodation
   payment by D/P   to inform you
   that we are ready

   _____
   _____

4. on the basis of D/A   to have you
   as one of our customers   to do business
   we would like   but
   we regret our inability

   _____
   _____

5. we are unable   any extension of import license
   of our L/C No.789   much to our regret

do not permit ... to comply with your request because the present import regulations ... for an extension

_____

_____

V. Translation.

1. The check for USD1,000 was returned by Chase Manhattan Bank for the reason of "non-sufficient funds".

_____

2. In the event of our acceptance of your offer, we shall open an irrevocable L/C in your favor, payable in China against shipping documents.

_____

3. The L/C procedure is being preceded by BOC.

_____

4. As requested in your fax of December 15, shipment of 500 mts of soybeans will be effected under guarantee in the absence of the L/C amendment. Please, therefore, honor the draft accordingly.

_____

_____

5. It will interest you to know that as a special sign of encouragement, we shall consider accepting payment by D/P during this sales-pushing stage.

_____

6. 请注意，付款是以保兑的、不可撤销的、允许分装和转船的、见票即付的信用证支付。

_____

7. 你方以付款交单方式付款的要求，我方予以考虑。鉴于这笔交易金额甚微，我们准备以此方式办理装运。

_____

8. 你方可能记得，按照我方第321号售货确认书规定，有关信用证应不迟于11月15日到达我处。因此，希望你方及时开证，以免耽误装运。

_____

9. 请注意第 268 号合约项下的 800 辆自行车已备妥待运,但我们尚未收到你方有关的信用证。请速开来,以便装运。
_____
_____

10. 现寄上邮政汇票 1 000 美元结清欠款。
_____
_____

VI. Complete the following letters with proper words.

Letter 1

Dear Sirs,

    We _____ an application form for documentary _____ and shall be glad if you will arrange to _____ for our account with your office in London an _____ letter of credit for $1,000 in _____ of the Urban Trading Company, the credit to be _____ until November 30.

    The credit which _____ shipment of 2,000 tons of steel may be used _____ presentation of the following _____: bills of _____ in _____, one copy of commercial _____, packing list, _____ of insurance and certificate of _____. The company may _____ on your London office at 60 days' _____ for each shipment.

Yours faithfully,

Letter 2

Dear Sirs,

    Thank you for your letter of 10 November, 2014.

    We have _____ your request for a _____ delivery of silver cutlery on documents against _____ terms, but _____ to say that we cannot _____ to your proposal.

    As an _____, the best we can do for the trial is to _____ you direct payment at sight terms.

    If you _____ our proposal you run very little risk, since our silver cutlery is well _____ for its quality, attractive design and reasonable _____. Our lines sell very well all over the world and have done so for the last 100 years. We do not think you will have any difficulty in _____ a satisfactory volume of _____.

    If you find our proposal _____, please let us know and we can then expedite the transaction.

Sincerely yours,

Letter 3

Dear Ms. Ni,
Order No. 9953

Thank you for your order which has been _____ and is being sent to you today.

As _____ we have forwarded our bill, No. 2782 for EUR1,720 with _____ to your bank, Industrial & Commercial Bank of China, Caohejing Branch, Shanghai. The draft has been _____ out for payment 30 days after _____, and the documents will be handed to you on _____.

Yours sincerely,

VII. Writing.

1. 根据下列提示写一封完整的买方回复函。

主题：有关 L/C No. 78967 上的错误
说明：由于这是一批紧急货物，我方将不修改信用证，但会指示银行接受你方瑕疵押汇文件。
结论：请确认并告知出货明细。

2. 根据下列提示写一封信用证修改函。

主题：感谢收到 L/C No. 880128，发现有误，请修改：
（1）价格条件应该是 FOB HK。
（2）应该允许转运。
（3）最后出货期应该是 10 月 3 日。
请尽快修改，并回电确认。

3. A foreign buyer whom you do not want to lose has purchased 2,000 pieces of cotton piece goods from you for delivery in September. As the goods are ready for shipment, write a letter to the buyer urging them to open the covering L/C immediately.

Chapter 12

Packing

> **Lead-in: Case Study**
>
> Having settled all the questions of price, quantity and payment regarding the transaction of ladies' pajamas, now you have to write a letter about your requirement of packing.
>
> (1) Refer to the packing matter.
>
> (2) Give the instructions of packing. Ten garments in a polybag and twenty-five bags in a carton. Besides, you should emphasize that the usual ways of packing for garments is to use cartons and give the substantial reasons why you use the cartons.
>
> (3) Hope for earliest reply.

扫描二维码
自学 PPT

The goods will have to travel a long distance to reach the clients abroad. A good handle of the packing will earn you not only the profits but also the clients. The general principle in packing is to make sure that the goods are secured for the long journey and kept as small and light as possible.

There are 3 main packing methods: bulk packing/outer packing, small packing/inner packing and individual packing. When writing a packing instruction, you should write as explicitly as possible, not only outer packing but also inner packing. Outer packing is used for the convenience of protection and transportation of the goods while inner packing is designed for the promotion of sales. The goods should be packed in a way according to the importer's instruction or the trade custom without violating the importing country's regulations on outer packing material, length and weight, or going against the importing country's social customs and national preference for inner packing colors and designs, etc. To facilitate the identification of goods, the outer packing must be marked clearly with identifying symbols and numbers which should be the same as indicated in the commercial invoice, the bill of lading and the other shipping documents. The packing list should be provided in the foreign trade.

Marks include main mark, which must indicate the destination, carton number and country of origin, and side mark, which must clearly show the quantity, net weight and gross weight.

Marks can be generally divided into two kinds, shipping mark or simply known as mark, and indicative and warning mark. Shipping mark is usually a symbol consisting of the name or initials of the consignee or shipper, destination and packaging number, etc. Indicative and warning mark gives handling instructions in words or by internationally recognized symbols, such as "Do Not Drop" "This Side Up" "Keep Dry" "Handle with Care" and so on. Apart from these two kinds of marks, there may be some other marks to indicate dimensions and weight.

The nowadays packing containers are plastic bag, box, carton, wooden case, crate, pallet, foamed polystyrene, air bubbles plastic sheet, and container.

In a letter about packing, the instructions must be given in a very specific way so that the other party can fully comprehend and follow the instructions. At the same time, letters regarding packing will cover the packing methods, quantity, size, weight, as well as whether the packing meets the needs or there are any improvements.

扫描二维码
阅读了解
"How to Pack?"

Sample 1: Stating Packing Requirements

May 20, 2016
To: Mr. Folk
From: Tang Wanliang

Dear Mr. Folk,

On May 19, we received your consignment of 40 cardboard cartons of steel screws.

We regret to inform you that 10 cartons were delivered damaged and the contents had spilled, leading to some losses.

We accept that the damage was not your fault but feel that we must modify our packing requirements to avoid future losses.

We require that future packing be in wooden boxes of 20 kilos net, each wooden box containing 40 cardboard packs of 500 grams net.

Please let us know whether you can meet these specifications and whether they will lead to an increase in your prices.

We look forward to your early confirmation.

Sincerely yours,
Tang Wanliang
Overseas Sales Director

Sample 2: Stating Marking Requirements

October 27, 2016
To: James Sen
From: Hamzza A. Sesay

Dear James,

  The countersigned copy of contract No. 250 of October 3, 2016 for 300 pairs of shoes is enclosed.

  The letter of credit is on its way to you.

  Please mark the cartons in diamond with our initials, the destination and contract number are as follows:

$$\diamondsuit \begin{array}{c} \text{SSD} \\ \text{Tokyo} \\ \text{250} \end{array}$$

  The mark will apply to all shipments unless otherwise instructed.

  Please advise us by fax as soon as the shipment is effected.

Yours faithfully,
Hamzza A. Sesay
Managing Director

Sample 3: Packing Proposal from the Buyer

July 25, 2016
To: Mr. Wang
From: Leonardo

Dear Mr. Wang,

  We refer to our order for 500 dozen pairs of Lee jeans and your sales confirmation No. 225.

  Particular care should be taken to the packing of the goods to be delivered in the first order. It is the usual practice here that 10 shirts are packed to a carton and 10 cartons to a strong seaworthy wooden case. There will be a flow of orders if this initial order proves to be satisfactory.

  We are enclosing our confirmation of purchase.

  We trust this order will be the first of a series of deals between us.

Sincerely yours,
Leonardo
Department Three

Sample 4: Buyer's Response to Packing

July 15, 2016
To: Mike
From: Bill
Re: Packing for Ready-made Blouse

Dear Mike,

We have approached our clients about packing after receiving your letter of July 10. After our repeated explanation, they accept your packing of the blouse in cartons if you guarantee that you will pay compensation in all cases wherein they cannot indemnify from the insurance company for the reason that the cartons are not seaworthy.

We must remind you that should the insurance company refuse compensation, you would hold yourselves responsible for the losses. Our clients might sustain on account of your use of such cartons.

We hope you can understand our candid statement is made for our mutual benefits, as packing is a sensitive subject, which often leads to trade dispute.

We appreciate your cooperation.

Yours sincerely,
Bill
Import Department

Sample 5: Amending for Packing and Marking

June 7, 2016
To: Mr. Fang
From: Picker
Re: S/C No. 800918 for Packing

Dear Mr. Fang,

We have found that the packing clause is not so clear. The relative clause reads as, "Packing: seaworthy export packing, suitable for long distance ocean transportation."

In order to eliminate possible future trouble, we should like to make clear beforehand our packing requirements as follows:

The tea under the captioned contract should be packed in international standard tin boxes, 24 boxes to a pallet, 10 pallets in a FCL container. On the outer packing, please make our initials JGT in a diamond, under which the port of destination and our order number should be stenciled. In addition, warning marks should also be indicated.

> We look forward to your reply.
>
> Yours sincerely,
Picker
General Manager

Sample 6: Informing the Details of the Packing

> May 4, 2016
> **To:** Mr. Augustatos
> **From:** Geng Shuying
>
> Dear Mr. Augustatos,
>
>   The consignment you ordered is dispatched today, and should arrive within three weeks.
>
>   The engine parts have been wrapped in waterproof material and packed into crates. Carburetor units have been packed separately into boxes attached into crates to the side of each crate. Lifting hooks are provided at four points. These crates are non-returnable.
>
>   The generator has been bolted into specially made crates and surrounded by hard padding. These have lifting hooks at two points. A charge of $120 has been made on each of these crates, which is repayable if you return them in reasonable condition.
>
> Yours sincerely,
Geng Shuying
Export Manager

1. Supplementary Information

1) Mark Samples

Main Mark	Side Mark
BM NEW YORK C/NO. 1-100 MADE IN THAILAND	586 Notebook Computer **QTY:** 2 set **NW:** 20 kgs **GW:** 24 kgs

2) Packing Materials

(1) Bale: a package of soft goods (cotton, wool, sheepskin) tightly pressed together and wrapped in a protective material. Usual size may be strengthened by metal bands.

(2) Carton: made of light but strong cardboard, or fiberboard with double lids and bottoms, fixed by glue, adhesive tapes, metal bands or wire staples. Sometimes a bundle of several cartons is made up into one package, held by metal bands.

(3) Container. There are 3 types of container, general cargo container, specific cargo container, air freight container. Usually there are twenty-foot container and forty-foot container. The container service has the following advantages. Containers can be loaded and locked at factory premises or at nearby container bases, making pilferage impossible; There is no risk of goods getting lost or mislaid in transit; Manpower in handling is reduced, with lower costs and less risk of damage; Mechanical handling enables cargoes to be loaded in a matter of hours rather than days, thus reducing the time ships spend in port and greatly increasing the number of sailings; Temperature controlled containers are provided for the types of cargo that need them. The popular used term of FCL is a short form for full container load and LCL for less than container load.

扫描二维码
浏览视频
"Introduction to Trailer and Container"

(4) Crate: a case not fully enclosed. Crates are built for the particular thing they have to carry. Machinery packed in a crate needs a special bottom to facilitate handling.

3) Packing Documents
(1) Packing list（装箱单）
(2) Weight list（重量单）
(3) Measurement list（尺码单）

2. Useful Expression

(1) *The 0.5 litre tins of paint will be supplied in strong cardboard cartons, each containing 48 tins, with a gross weight of 50 kg.*

(2) *All export bicycles are wrapped in strong waterproof material at the port and packed in pairs in lightweight crates.*

(3) *We will pack the material in bales of 2 metres in length and 3 metres in girth. The protective canvas will be provided with ears to facilitate lifting.*

(4) *We pack our shirts in plastic-lined, waterproof cartons, reinforced with metal traps.*

(5) *A special crate with reinforced bottom will be needed for the transport of such a large machine, and both padding and bolting down will be essential.*

(6) *We object to packing in cartons unless the flaps are glued down and the cartons secured by metal bands.*

(7) *Our usual packing for dyed poplin is in bales lined with water proof paper, each containing 500 yards in single color.*

(8) *Our usual packing for tea has proven successful for a long time in many export shipment.*

(9) *The great care must be given to packing as any damage in transit would result in a great loss.*

(10) *The careful consideration has been taken into packing. We have improved it so as to avoid damage to the goods.*

(11) *Please limit the weight of any one carton to 10 kg and metal-strap all cartons in stacks of 4.*

(12) *Please cut vent-holes in the cases to minimize condensation.*

(13) *Please note that the packing we require is 6pcs in an inner box and 6 boxes in an export carton.*

(14) *We require that future packing be in wooden boxes of 20 kilos net, each wooden box containing 40 cardboard packs of 500 grams net.*

(15) *We provide both 20 and 40 foot containers. They open at both ends, thus facilitating loading and unloading.*

(16) *For goods liable to be spoiled by damp or water, our containers have the advantage of being watertight and airtight.*

Exercises

I. **Choose the appropriate word or words to complete the sentences.**

1. We regret that we have suffered heavy loss (resulted in, resulted from, resulting in, resulting from) your improper packing.
2. We would suggest that you (secure, will secure, securing, are secured) the carton with double straps.
3. Metal handles should be fixed to the boxes to (make, convenience, easy, facilitate) carrying.
4. We give you on the attached sheet full details regarding packing and marking, which must be strictly (observed, abide by, signified, submitted).
5. Your comments on packing will (be passed, passed, be passing, passing) on to our manufactures for their reference.
6. This container can be easily opened (on, at, in, by) both ends.
7. We give you on the attached full details (regarded, regarding, be regarded, regard) packing and marking,
8. Taking into consideration the transport condition (in, on, with, at) your end, we have improved our packing so as to avoid damage to the goods.

II. **Fill in the blanks.**

1. Packing _____ sturdy wooden cases is essential. Cases must be nailed, battered and cured by overall, mental strapping.
2. The greatest care must be _____ to packing and crating as any damage in transit would cause us heavy losses.

3. As the goods will probably be _____ to a thorough examination, the cases should be of a type which can be made fast again after opening.
4. Our cartons for canned food are not only seaworthy but also strong enough to protect the goods from possible _____.
5. Each jar is wrapped in tissue paper before being _____ into its individual decorative cardboard box.
6. We understand your concern about packing, and can assure you that we take every possible precaution to ensure that our products _____ our customers in prime condition.
7. The boxes are packed in strong cardboard cartons, 12 _____ a carton, separated from each other by paper dividers.
8. Since the crates are specially made to _____ 24 cartons, there is no danger of movements inside them.
9. The crates are lined with waterproof, airtight material. The lids are secured by nailing, and the crates are _____ with metal bands.
10. Since cartons are comparatively light and compact, they are more convenient to handle in the _____ of loading and unloading.

III. Give the English or Chinese equivalents of the followings.

1. 修改包装指令   _____
2. 包装条款   _____
3. 包装不妥   _____
4. 适合海运的包装   _____
5. 防水防潮   _____
6. to coat with anti-rust grease   _____
7. to pack in spear/in block/in slice/in bulk   _____
8. padding   _____
9. carton label   _____
10. to line with craft paper   _____

IV. Arrange the following words and phrases in their proper order.

1. please   in strong polythene bags
   if cartons are used   each chemical
   ensure to   supply
   protection from damp

   _____

2. reinforced by battens   as the former
   a light case   would be non-returnable
   and be much cheaper   than a solid wooden case
   would meet your requirements

3. when   of suitable size
   the various items   of your order
   into handles   in our warehouse
   for shipment   are complete
   we will pack them

4. covered with waterproof fabric   please make our order up
   and strapped into bales   of about 200kg each
   with metal bands   horizontally
                                    and vertically

5. of the machine   against the container
   and generously padded   to avoid
   are to be wrapped   all polished parts
   knocking and scratching

V. Translation.

1. The packing of our men's shirt is each in a poly bag, 5 dozens to a carton lined with waterproof paper and bound with two iron straps outside.

2. Our cotton prints are packed in cases lined with draft paper and waterproof paper, each consisting of 30 pieces in one design with 5 color ways equally assorted.

3. Glass wares are fragile goods. They need special packing precautions against jotting.

4. Please note the packing is 5pcs in an inner box, 10 boxes in an export carton, 6 cartons in a pallet.

5. 我们高兴地通知贵公司，现可以接受按买方指定的图纸和包装的订单。

6. 雪茄烟每5支装一包，20包装一条，144条装一纸箱。

7. 集装箱的防水和密封设计能够避免货物受潮导致的损坏。

VI. Writing.

1. Write a letter to your customer telling him that you have improved your packing and that from now on all garments are to be packed in cartons instead of wooden cases.

2. 根据下列提示写出货包装函。

> 先生：
> 　　请注意我们要求的包装是10个装一个内盒，10盒装一个外箱。
> 　　此外请和以前出货一样用直飞方式空运给我们，并使用空运授权编号82028。
> 　　请按上述包装方式包装，并尽快告知出货明细。

VII. Complete the following letters with proper words.

Letter 1

Dear Sirs,

The 12,000 cycles you ordered will be _____ for dispatch by February 17. Since you require them for onward _____ to Bahrain, Kuwait, Oman and Qatar, we are arranging for them to be _____ in seaworthy containers.

Each bicycle is enclosed in a corrugated cardboard pack, and 20 are banded together and _____ in sheet plastic. A container holds 240 cycles; the whole cargo would therefore comprise 50 containers, each weighing 8 tons. _____ can be made from our works by rail to be forwarded from Shanghai harbor. The freight _____ from works to Shanghai are $80 per container, totally $4,000 for this _____, excluding container hire, which will be charged to your account.

Please let us have your delivery _____.

Yours faithfully,

Letter 2

Dear Sirs,

We would refer to our order No. 120 of August 15 for machine tools. Please now _____ the first part of this order (items 1-8) by air, as these are urgently _____ by customers. We suggest the use of cartons with hinged lids to _____ opening for customs examination.

You will no doubt _____ with your arrangements for transport by sea for the reminder of the consignment, and we would ask you to be particularly careful to seal each box _____ a watertight bag—we recommend plastic—before packing into cases. In your last consignment, we were obliged to remove a certain amount of rust, which we presume had formed during the _____.

Yours sincerely,

Letter 3

Dear Sirs,

Your consignment of chemicals is now _____ for dispatch, and we are arranging _____ by S.S. "Yamagawa Maru", sailing from Shanghai on May 24.

The sulphuric acid is supplied in thirty 4-gallon carboys, doubled-packaged for extra safety, and with a protective lid to _____ breakage of the mouth. The ammonia is in forty 5-cwt steel drums.

Please _____ safe arrival of the consignment.

Yours sincerely,

Chapter 13

Shipping

> **Lead-in: Case Study**
>
> Your company has purchased 2,000 raincoats from Harding&Co. of Hull under order No.3321. The selling season is approaching, but you haven't got any information about the effect of shipment. Write a letter to Harding & Co. of Hull to urge shipment with the following points:
>
> (1) The relevant L/C has been extended to 31st May.
>
> (2) The season is approaching; buyers are badly in need of the goods to catch the brisk demand of the selling season.
>
> (3) Any delay in shipment will cause lots of difficulties.

In shipping goods abroad, the dealer has various alternative methods which include ship, truck, rail, air and parcel post.

The choice will depend on the nature of the product (light or heavy, fragile or sturdy, perishable or durable, high or low in value per cubic meter, etc); the distance to be shipped; available means of transportation; and relative freight costs.

For goods having high weight or cubic capacity or value ratio, the usual method of shipping overseas is by ocean cargo vessel. However, when speed is essential, air cargo may be preferred, although more expensive. For example, ski jackets are shipped from Germany to Japan by sea but towards the end of the ski season, air cargo is used.

Shipment is mostly made by ocean vessel, which is the most economical means compared with other forms of transport such as overland transport, and air transport and usually involves tramp, liner or container. The contract between the ship-owner and shipper may take the form of either a charter party or a B/L. When goods are shipped by road, rail or air, the contract of carriage takes the form of consignment note or air way bill. To ensure prompt delivery of the ordered goods in satisfactory manner, the parties concerned, including the consignor, the carrier, and the consignee

扫描二维码
自学 PPT

should stay in frequent contact.

Shipment is a complicated process. Before shipment, the buyer generally sends the shipping requirement to the seller, informing the way of packing and the relevant information, known as the shipping instructions. As to the shipping advice, it is usually sent from the seller to the buyer immediately after the goods are loaded on the vehicle to advise the shipment.

Letters regarding shipment are usually written for the following purposes: to urge an early shipment, to amend shipping terms, to give shipping advice, to dispatch shipping documents and so on.

Sample 1: Asking for the Transportation Method

May 19, 2016
To: Mr. Esses
From: Picker

Dear Mr. Esses,

I am pleased to receive your order for our livestock and I will be pleased to send these to you in 5 weeks' time as arranged.

We'd like to know how you want to transport the current order of small tropical fish. As explained in our catalog, the fish are packed in special insulated plastic containers which should keep them in good condition for up to thirty days after leaving here. We can send them by air or by sea—as you wish, but by air the cost of carriage, which we will invoice to you, will be increased by 50%—from £80 to £120.

As you know, you have also ordered some pythons later in the year. These will travel much more easily in the large reinforced crates. They simply go to sleep if the temperature falls.

Please let us know the method of transport you prefer for both consignments.

Sincerely,
Picker
Export Manager

Sample 2: Informing the Transportation Method

September 19, 2016
To: Ms Lee
From: Train Tata
Re: P/O 10003

Dear Ms Lee,

Please note that the packing is 6 pcs in an inner box and 6 boxes in an export carton.

Also, please ship this order the same as previous shipments by direct air to us, and use air authorized code #6785.

Please follow the above packing instructions and advise shipping details soon.

Sincerely,
Train Tata

Sample 3: Advising Partial Shipment

June 6, 2016
To: Mr. Augustatos
From: Geng Shuying

Dear Mr. Augustatos,

We have shipped, in partial fulfillment of your order No. 685, five sets of NY565 milling machines per S.S. *Five Star* which sailed today.

We enclosed all the copy documents.

As for the remaining 6 sets, we will endeavor to advance shipment and will advise you as soon as it is effected.

We appreciate the business you have secured for us. All further inquires and orders will continue to receive our prompt and careful attention.

Yours sincerely,
Geng Shuying

Sample 4: Urging an Early Shipment

March 20, 2016
To: Helen
From: Tang Wanliang
Re: Our Purchase Contract No. 885

Dear Helen,

We wish to remind you that we have had no news from you about shipment of the goods.

As mentioned in our last letter, we are in urgent need of the goods and we may be compelled to seek an alternative source of supply.

Under the circumstances, it is not possible for us to extend further our letter of credit No. 562 which will expire on May 21. Please understand how serious and urgent it is for us to resolve this matter.

We look forward to receiving your shipping advice.

Sincerely,
Tang Wanliang
Overseas Sales Director

Sample 5: Giving Shipping Advice

July 15, 2016
To: Mike
From: Bill D. H.

扫描二维码
阅读了解
"Shipment Advice"

Dear Mike,

We are pleased to inform you that the Teddy Bear you ordered on May 25 will be shipped by S.S. *Maria*, which is scheduled to leave for Guangzhou on July 30.

We enclose our invoice and shall present shipping documents and our draft for acceptance through the CitiBank, Guangzhou Office, as agreed.

When the goods reach you, we trust you will be completely satisfied with them. We look forward to further orders from you.

Sincerely,
Bill D. H.

扫描二维码
阅读了解
"How to Write a Perfect Shipping Advice"

Sample 6: Amending Shipping Terms

October 27, 2016
To: Mike
From: Hamzza A. Sesay
Re: Shipment of L/C 2324N02

Dear Mike,

We are sorry for the delay in the shipment, as there is no vessel available this week. The soonest vessel will be early next week. So, please amend/extend the latest shipping date to November 11 and the expiry date to November 30, 2016.

Also, please E-mail us your inspection standard and confirm if every piece packed in a blister is OK.

Yours faithfully,
Hamzza A. Sesay
Managing Director

Chapter 13　Shipping

1. Supplementary Information
1) Four Main Methods of Transporting Goods

(1) Road transport tends to be comparatively cheaper and more direct than rail, and in the past few years, haulage has doubled in many countries. The reasons for this include the increased capacity for lorries to carry goods, particularly with the introduction of containers, faster services, road improvements, and ferries offering rolling-on and rolling-off facilities.

(2) Rail transport is faster than road transport, which is necessary especially when transporting perishable goods, such as fish, fruit, meat, and can haul bulk commodities in greater volume than road transport. Nevertheless, rail transport tends to be comparatively more expensive than road haulage.

(3) Air transport has the advantages of saving time, particularly over long distances. Insurance also tends to be cheaper as consignments spend less time in transit. However, with bulky, cumbersome equipment and bulk commodities, air transport is much more expensive.

(4) Sea transport is the most widely used of the four forms of transportation in international trade. It is generally considered to be a cheap mode of transport for delivering large quantities of goods over long distances.

2) Shipping Procedure

The following steps are involved in a typical overseas shipping procedure.

(1) The freight forwarder is advised of the export order.

(2) The terms of sale are examined to determine the exporter's shipping responsibility and ability to fill the order.

(3) If the letter of credit is involved, it must also be carefully examined to insure that any shipping conditions (shipping date, no partial shipments, discharge port, transshipment restrictions) are met or, if impossible to meet, arrangements should be made for the letter of credit to be amended.

(4) Quotations on freight rates sought from different shipping agents.

(5) A shipping line and vessel are selected.

(6) Space is booked as early as possible (as shipping space is not easily available to all destinations) through a shipping agent. The space should be on a ship with an acceptable loading port and acceptable estimated time of arrival (or ETA) at the required port of destination.

3) Knowledge of Shipment

The choice of loading port must be balanced against the preferred date of sailing. Information about sailing schedules is available in specialized shipping publications and in the business sections of the major newspapers.

The agent that represents the shipping line will, in booking the space, requires full details of the shipment, including weight, size, contents value, ports of shipment and destination. This is recorded by the exporter onto a shipping note that is sent to the steamship office.

The shipping agent then sends the exporter a contract number and an engagement note showing the details of the shipment, including the name of the ship, destination, loading port, loading date, arrival date, and the shipping rate.

The exporter may cancel the space that has been reserved if the export order falls through. However, it should let the shipping company know as soon as possible so that the space can be allocated to someone else. Otherwise the shipping company will invoice the exporter for the unused space.

(1) Customs forms are filled out for the country of destination.

(2) The shipment is appropriately packaged and marked.

(3) Wait for the "calling forward" notice from the shipping company.

(4) The shipment is dispatched to the port with a consignment note.

(5) A bill of lading is obtained from the shipping company and freight charges are paid.

(6) The bill of lading and other required documents are delivered to the bank for collection.

4) Tramp and Liner

A tramp is a freight-carrying vessel, which has no regular route or schedule of sailings. It is first in one trade and then in another, always seeking those ports where there is demand at the moment for shipping space.

A liner is a vessel with regular sailings and arrivals on a stated schedule between specified ports.

5) Bill of Lading

扫描二维码
阅读了解"B/L"

(1) Definition: in Hamburg Rules, B/L means a document which evidences a contract of carriage by sea and the taking over or loading of the goods by the carrier, and by which the carrier undertakes to deliver the goods against surrender of the documents. A provision in the document that the goods are to be delivered to the order of a named person, or to order, or to bearer, constitutes such an undertaking.

(2) Function: a receipt for the goods, an evidence of the contract of carriage, a document of title.

(3) Classification: shipped on board B/L and received for shipment B/L; clean B/L and unclean B/L; in apparent good order; direct/with transshipment/through B/L.

6) Services Offered by the Freight Forwarder

Freight forwarder can offer a variety of services: advising on the best routes and relative shipping costs; booking the necessary space with the shipping or airline; arranging with the exporter for packing and marking of the goods; consolidating shipments from different exporters; handling customs clearance abroad; arranging marine insurance for the shipment; preparing the export documentation; translating foreign language correspondence; scrutinizing and advising on ability to comply with letters of credit.

7) Manufacturers' Certificate of Quality

Manufacturers' certificate of quality is one of the quality certificates acceptable. The rests are quality certificate issued by Bureau of Commodity Inspection and Quarantine, quality certificate issued by an independent public survey, and quality certificate issued by agent. It is best that the manufacturer will be able to issue the certificate since it can fulfill the 100% testing experiment, or it has been awarded by ISO, UL, CE, FCC. The goods tested by Bureau of Commodity Inspection and Quarantine, an independent public survey, or agent will adhere to AQL (acceptable quality level), which can not be guaranteed with 100% approved quality.

8) S.S.

S.S. is the abbreviation of "steam ship". We also have M.V., which is the abbreviation of "motor vessel". There are several modes of shipment, including direct shipment, indirect shipment, partial shipment, and transshipment.

2. Useful Expression

(1) *The shipment is stated with a fixed date, for examples, shipment during January, shipment at/before the end of March, shipment on/before May 15th, shipment during April/May.*

(2) *An indefinite date of shipment is stipulated depending on certain conditions such as shipment within 30 days after receipt of L/C, shipment subject to shipping space available, shipment by the first available steamer.*

(3) *The shipment is indicated with a date in the near future usually in such terms as immediate shipment, prompt shipment, and shipment as soon as possible, but without unified interpretation as to their definite time limit. It is advisable to avoid using these ambiguous terms.*

(4) *We will ship by the first steamer available next month.*

(5) *We are able to effect shipment within one month after your order has been confirmed.*

(6) *To repack the goods would involve a delay of about 2 weeks in shipment.*

(7) *The goods have long been ready for shipment, but owing to the late arrival of your L/C, the shipment can hardly be effected as anticipated.*

(8) *We regret that we are unable to meet your need for advancing the shipment to November.*

(9) *We look forward to your prompt shipment./The shipment shall be effected as soon as possible./Immediate delivery would be required.*

(10) *Please let us know when you could manage to ship the goods.*

(11) *Shipment is to be made in May/within 3 days/in the first half of March.*

(12) *It has to be stressed that shipment must be made within the prescribed time limit, as a further extension will not be considered by our end-user.*

(13) *It is fixed that shipment to be made before the end of this month and, if*

possible, we should appreciate your arranging to ship the goods at an earlier date.

(14) *We have pleasure in advising that we have completed the above shipment according to the stipulations set forth in L/C No.567.*

(15) *All your orders booked up to date have been executed.*

(16) *We wish to draw your attention to the fact that the goods have been ready for shipment for a long time and the covering L/C, due to arrive here before March 13, has not been received up to now. Please let us know the reason for the delay.*

(17) *As there is no direct sailing from Shanghai to your port during April/May, it is imperative for you to delete the clause "by direct steamer" and insert the wording "partial shipment and transshipment are allowed".*

(18) *As the cargo is to be transshipped at HK, we shall require through Bs/L.*

(19) *Your instructions as to marking have been accurately carried out and the goods packed with all the care of our experienced dispatch staff.*

(20) *In view of the fragile nature of the goods, we require them to be forwarded by air, and we would therefore be glad to know the lowest rates.*

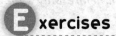xercises

I. **Correct inappropriate words and expressions.**

1. Only by the end of the next month, the goods can be packed ready for delivery.
2. Having no direct steamer to your port from Dalian, the goods have to be transshipped at Hong Kong.
3. Please send us full instructions for the ten cases for London such as contents, value, consignee and who pays all the charges.
4. All powders are wrapped in plastic bags and packed in tins, which the lids are sealed with adhesive tape.
5. As requested, we are already carried out marking and numbering on all cases.
6. For the boxes are possible to receive rough handling at this end, you must see to it that packing is strong enough to protect goods.
7. In order that we facilitate to sell, it would be better to pack the goods in cases of 50 dozen each equally.
8. We would ask you to do everything probable ensuring punctual shipment.

II. **Fill in the blanks.**

1. We regret our _____ to comply with your request for shipping the goods in early May.

2. We have the pleasure of informing you that the _____ has gone per S.S. "East Wind" and hope it will arrive at the destination in perfect condition.
3. Shipping shall be _____ within 40 days.
4. Before deciding which form of transport to use, a _____ will take into account the factors of cost, speed and safety.
5. Some parts of the machine susceptible to shock must be packed in seaworthy cases capable of withstanding rough _____.
6. In order to ensure the earlier shipment, we would like to make this an _____ and agree to transshipment.
7. Goods sold shall be guaranteed by the seller to _____ to the sample arrival at destinations.
8. The consignment will be sent _____ to reach the final destination by the end of March.
9. This is to certify that the goods _____ by this invoice are neither of Republic of Korea nor of Singapore.
10. Even though the goods are ready, we don't know whether we can _____ the shipping space immediately.

III. **Give the English or Chinese equivalents of the following.**

1. 提前装运　　　　　_____
2. 搬运不当　　　　　_____
3. 包机　　　　　　　_____
4. 装卸日期　　　　　_____
5. 舱位　　　　　　　_____
6. weight memo 　　　_____
7. forwarding agent 　_____
8. to reach in good order _____
9. initial shipment 　　_____
10. dead freight 　　　_____

IV. **Arrange the following words and phrases in their proper order.**

1. in accordance with your instructions　　your order No. 32
   to inform you that　　　　　　　　　　we are pleased
   packed in twelve 100 kg cases　　　　　has been dispatched

_____
_____
_____

2. the order   it should reach you tomorrow
   today   so that
   in view of the urgency of   we have dispatched
   by air   the goods

   _____

   _____

3. in the case of   are subject to
   without prior notice   our rates
   except   special contract
   alteration

   _____

   _____

4. and method of transport   you wish to export
   for any country   on suitable packing
   and as a result of   we can advise you
   our wide experience

   _____

   _____

5. in one of our previous letters   are in urgent need
   for an early delivery   as you have been informed
   the users   and in fact are pressing us
   of the machines contracted

   _____

   _____

V. Complete the following sentences in English.

1. Please send us your shipping instructions
   a. 以便我们备货装船。

   _____

   b. 以便我们租订舱位。

   _____

c. 以便我们办理海关手续。

2. According to the contract stipulations
   a. 唛头由买方选定。

   b. 卖方必须在 9 月内完成货物的装运工作。

3. We prefer
   a. 装直达轮，而不在新加坡转船。

   b. 货物用木箱包装，箱净重 100 千克，不用双层麻袋包装。

   c. 采用付款交单方式，而不采用 60 天期汇票支付。

4. It is expressly stated that
   a. 货物必须于 10 月底以前装船。

   b. 500 公吨花生应于 9 月装运，其余 500 公吨于 10 月装运。

   c. 1,000 公吨花生必须一次装船。

VI. Complete the following letters with proper words.

Letter 1

Dear Sirs,

We are p_____ to confirm that the 100 compass power switches under your order No. JY-120 are now ready for s_____. When p_____ your order stressed the importance of p_____ delivery and we are g_____ to say that by m_____ a special effort we have been able to improve o_____ the delivery a few days a_____ of the time agreed upon.

We now await your shipping instructions and immediately we receive them, we shall send you our shipping a_____.

We look forward to your e_____ reply.

Yours faithfully,

Letter 2

Dear Sirs,

  We feel it n_____ to invite your a_____ to the subject order concluded with you last September and accepted by you in your letter of October 2, 2016, with w_____ a countersigned copy of the contract was enclosed.

  According to the s_____ schedule in the contract, two thirds of the order was to be shipped by the end of December, the b_____ to follow in February this year. We are, however, very much d_____ to have received no news f_____ you about the first shipment. And, w_____ is more, you haven't even r_____ to our fax of October 10, 2016.

  We anxiously await your reply soon.

Yours sincerely,

Letter 3

Dear Sirs,

  Referring _____ our previous letters, we wish to call your _____ to the fact that _____ to the present moment no _____ has come from you about the _____ under the contract.

  As you have been _____ in one of our previous letters, the users are in urgent _____ of the machines _____ and are in fact pressing us for assurance of an _____ delivery.

  Under the circumstances, it is obviously impossible for us to again _____ L/C No. 123456, which _____ on August 24, and we feel it is our duty to remind you _____ this matter again.

  As your prompt attention to shipment is most _____ to all parties _____, we hope you will fax us your shipping _____ without further delay.

Yours truly,

VII. Writing.

1. Write to a firm of shipping agents asking them to arrange for consignment to be collected from your factory and make all arrangements for transportation. Include imaginary particulars as to nature of consignment, names and addresses of consignors and consignee, and say who will take delivery of the consignment upon arrival.
2. As the secretary of Harding & Co. of Hull, write to Scandinavian Liners Ltd. for details of their sailings to Norway and Sweden and for quotations of their rates for manufactured woolen goods.

Chapter 14

Insurance

> **Lead-in: Case Study**
>
> You have covered on the goods with PICC Tianjin Branch against all risks for $480,000. Your cargo is expected to be delivered by S.S. Dongfeng, which will sail from Tianjin on or before July, 15. Write a letter about insurance to your customer, Mr. Smith of Petty Clothing Ltd., 623 Delhi Road, Bombay, India. Please enclose the relevant insurance policy together with your debit note for the premium.

Insurance is closely related to foreign trade. In international business, the transportation of the goods from the seller to the buyer is usually over a long distance and has to go through the procedures of loading, unloading and storing. This process involves various risks, which may result in the damage or loss of the goods, and thus the inconveniences or even financial losses to both the seller and the buyer. To protect the goods against possible losses, before shipment, the buyer or the seller usually applies to an insurance company for insurance covering the goods to be transported. Then where can you get the cargo insurance?

扫描二维码
自学 PPT

A specialist cargo insurance broker will find you a good price, ensure the cover suits your needs and help you with claims; some banks offer cargo insurance as part of a finance package. You can also ask your freight forwarder for a quote, but research suggests that their costs and service don't match those offered by specialist brokers. You need to be aware that carriers, freight forwarders or third-party service suppliers will not automatically insure goods that are under their care or control. They can only do so if instructed in writing.

The party who bears the obligation of insuring the goods under the sales contract, who is the exporter or the importer, arranges cargo insurance. Many exporters would like to arrange insurance and freight but pass on the cost to the buyer. However, the experts believe that which is better depends.

The exporter has greater control over the risk and could win business from competitors who do not offer insurance if he offers. Besides, if you leave your buyer to arrange insurance, they will do so before paying for the goods. You may not be paid in full if there's a problem and they're not adequately insured. In addition, if the goods are rejected when they get to the port of entry or to the customer's premises, they won't be covered by insurance, and the responsibility will be back with you.

The importer will minimize the risks if he arranges insurance of goods. He'll know how much he is paying and what's included. His supplier might not be able to give him full details of insurance cover, or if they do, the information may not be entirely reliable.

There are three sets of standard clauses published by the Institute of London Underwriters.

(1) Institute Cargo Clauses I (FPA, free of particular average).

(2) Institute Cargo Clauses II (WPA, with particular average).

(3) Institute Cargo Clauses III (all risks).

In addition, three new sets of clauses are also used.

(1) Institute Cargo Clauses (C) (almost equivalent to I above).

(2) Institute Cargo Clauses (B) (almost equivalent to II above).

(3) Institute Cargo Clauses (A) (almost equivalent to III above).

When you write a letter of covering insurance, see to it that you should write down clearly the following information: subject matter, duration of coverage, insurance amount and premium, scope of cover, etc.

Sample 1: Asking the Buyer to Cover Insurance

March 20, 2016
To: Mark
From: Tang Wanliang

Dear Mark,

Refer to your purchase order No. 885 for 1,000 sets of TCL color television.

We have booked shipping space for the consignment on S.S. Ocean Trader which sails for your port on or about June 1.

We would be grateful if you could arrange insurance cover for the consignment at your end.

Please telex your confirmation as soon as possible.

Sincerely yours,
Tang Wanliang
Overseas Sales Director

Sample 2: Asking the Seller to Cover the Insurance

October 27, 2016

To: Mr. Kum

From: Hamzza A. Sesay

Re: Our Order No. 321 for 30 Cases of Assorted Canned Food

Dear Mr. Kum,

 We wish to refer you to our order No. 321 for 30 cases of assorted canned food, from which you will see that this order is placed on CFR basis.

 In order to save time and simplify procedures, we now desire to have the shipment insured at your end. We shall be pleased if you will arrange to insure the goods on our behalf against all risks for 110% of the full invoice value, i.e. $3,000. May we suggest that you follow our proposal?

 We shall, of course, refund you the premium upon receipt of your debit note, or, if you like, you may draw on us at sight for the amount required.

 We sincerely hope that our request will meet with your proposal.

Yours faithfully,
Hamzza A. Sesay
Managing Director

Sample 3: Response of Having Covered Insurance

October 28, 2016

To: Hamzza A. Sesay

From: Kum

Re: Your Order No. 321 for 30 Cases of Assorted Canned Food

Dear Sesay,

 We have received your letter requesting us to effect insurance on the captioned shipment for your account.

 We are glad to tell you that we have covered the above shipment against all risks for $3,000 with the Insurance Company of Seoul. The policy is being prepared accordingly and will be forwarded to you by the end of this week together with our debit note for the premium.

 For your reference, we are making arrangements to ship the 30 cases of assorted canned food by S.S. Princess, sailing on or about November 10.

Sincerely,
Kum
Manager

Sample 4: Stating Insurance Coverage

March 3, 2016
To: Mr. Green
From: Picker

Dear Mr. Green,

We refer to your order No. 339 for 200 CL500 VCRs.

We shall be shipping your order by S.S. Spring, due to leave here at the end of this week.

Unless you give contrary instructions, we will arrange an all risk insurance policy for the shipment. In our opinion, this type of cover is necessary for a cargo of this nature.

We look forward to your early reply.

Sincerely,

Picker

Sample 5: Informing the Insurance Rate

June 6, 2016
To: Mr. Augustatos
From: Geng Shuying

Dear Mr. Augustatos,

Thank you for your fax of May 25.

I am pleased to tell you that we can arrange an all risk open cover policy for jeans shipments to South Europe.

As you propose to ship regularly, we offer you a rate of 0.0045 for a total cover of $110,000. I am enclosing a block of declaration forms, and you would be required to submit one for each shipment, giving full details.

I look forward to receiving your confirmation.

Yours sincerely,

Geng Shuying

Sample 6: Answering a Request for Excessive Insurance

May 5, 2016
To: Mr. Wang
From: Leonardo

Dear Mr. Wang,

Thank you for your letter of May 1 referring to your order No. 811 for 5,000 sets of "Sea Gull" cameras.

Your request for insurance coverage up to the inland city is acceptable on condition that such extra premium is for your account.

But we cannot grant you insurance coverage for 125% of the invoice value, because the contract stipulates that insurance is to be covered for 110% of invoice value.

We trust that you will find this arrangement acceptable.

Sincerely yours,
Leonardo

1. Supplementary Information
1) Insurance Stages
The stages of arranging insurance cover are as follows.
(1) The party seeking cover completes a proposal form.
(2) The insurance company assesses the risk and fixed premium to be paid.
(3) The premium is paid and the cover starts.
(4) If a loss is suffered, the insured makes a claim for compensation.
(5) The claim is investigated, and if found to be valid, the compensation is paid.

2) Insurance Documents
The insurance policy is the principle document and is in fact a contract of indemnity. This is issued for each shipment that is made.

There is also a procedure of insurance often used now, known as open cover, by which there is a rather general arrangement between the insurer and the insured that the latter will have all consignments insured by the former.

3) Duration of Cover
The period covered by a marine cargo policy is defined as "warehouse to warehouse" in the transit clause of the Institute Cargo Clauses. Under this clause, the insurance attaches from the time when the goods leave the warehouse for the commencement of transit, continues during the ordinary course of transit, and terminates either on delivery to the final warehouse at destination or on the expiry of 60 days after completion of discharge, whichever shall first occur. It further provides to the effect that the insurance shall terminate on delivery to any other warehouse or place of storage, whether prior to or at the destination named in the policy, which the assured elects to use either for storage other than in the ordinary course of transit, or for allocation or distribution.

However, the duration of cover against war risk is limited to "waterborne", which means that the goods are covered against war risks only when they are on board the ocean going vessel.

4) Insured Value and Insured Amount

Since it is impracticable to assess the market value of the insured goods at the time and place when and where the loss of or damage to them takes place during the course of transit, an agreement on the valuation of the goods is made beforehand between the insurer and the assured when the contract of marine cargo insurance is concluded. Such value is called "agreed insured value" and the marine cargo insurance policy is called "valued policy".

The insured amount is the limit of the amount, for which the insurer is liable in respect of one accident, and insurance premiums are calculated upon this amount. Although the insured value and insured amount are different terminologies, the insured amount is normally fixed at the same as the insured value.

5) CIF Terms and Cargo Insurance

Under CIF terms, the exporter is bound to provide marine insurance covering the whole voyage up to the final destination and to furnish the importer with shipping documents including the insurance policy.

There is another type of contract called C&I (cargo insurance) contract which is considered to be a variation of the CIF contract. Under C&I contracts, ocean freight is excluded from the price of sales contract since it is payable at the destination by the buyer. However, the obligation of the exporter relating to insurance is identical to that of CIF contract.

6) FOB and C&F Contracts

Under FOB terms, the exporter is bound to load the goods onto the carrying vessel at his own cost and risk, but he does not need to arrange insurance to protect the interests of the importer, which will be insured by the importer. In the case of C&F contract, the position of the exporter relating to insurance is quite the same as FOB contract, since the insurance premium covering the ocean voyage is excluded from the price of sales contract. The difference between FOB and C&F contracts relates to whom the ocean freight is paid by. Under FOB and C&F contracts, the exporter has an obligation of sending a shipping advice to the importer immediately on completion of loading the cargo at the port of shipment, so that the importer may effect insurance without delay. But the exporter bears the risk before loading for which he will have to arrange insurance on his own behalf.

The importer's position regarding insurance protection under various trade terms is the reverse of the exporter's. The importer on CIF terms must rely upon the insurance arranged by the exporter, and on FOB or C&F terms, he has to effect insurance by himself.

扫描二维码
浏览视频
"Marine Insurance"

2. Useful Expression

(1) We have covered insurance on the 100 metric tons of wool for 110% of the invoice value against all risks.

(2) In the absence of definite instructions from our clients, we generally cover insurance against WPA and war risk; if you desire to cover FPA, please let us know in advance.

(3) For transactions concluded on CIF basis, we usually cover the insurance against all risks at invoice value plus 10% with the People's Insurance Company of China as per CIC of January 1.

(4) We can cover all basic risks as required as long as they are stipulated in the ocean marine cargo clauses of the Lloyd Insurance Company, London.

(5) Please see that the above mentioned goods should be covered for 150% of invoice value against all risks. We know that according to your usual practice, you insure the goods only for 10% above invoice value, therefore the extra premium will be for our account.

(6) We will effect insurance against the usual risks, for the value of the goods plus freight.

(7) We will effect insurance against all risks, charging premium and freight to the consignments.

(8) Owing to the fact that these bags have occasionally been dropped into the water during loading and unloading, the insurers have raised the premium to 5%. We are therefore of the opinion that it would be to your advantage to have WA cover instead of FPA.

(9) Owing to the risk of war, we cannot accept the insurance at the ordinary rate. At the same time, it would be to your advantage to have particular average cover.

(10) Please insure/cover us on the cargo listed on the attached sheet.

(11) As you will be placing regular orders with us, we suggest that we take out an open policy approximately $1,500,000 annually. The rate for insurance would be 46 per cent, and would cover all risks except war, warehouse to warehouse, on scheduled sailings.

(12) As you hold the policy, we should be grateful if you would take the matter up for us with the underwriters to ensure indemnification.

扫描二维码
阅读了解
"Glossary of
Marine Insurance
and Shipping
Terms"

Exercises

I. Correct inappropriate words and expressions.

1. The cargo is to be insured from warehouse to warehouse by all risks.

2. As requested, we have covered insurance with 20,000 transistor radios at 10% above the invoice value for all risks.
3. Unless we hear from you on the contrary before the end of this month, we shall arrange to cover the goods against FPA for the value of the goods plus freight.
4. As concerned foreign trade, the following three risks cover an insurance policy, namely, FPA, WPA and all risks.
5. If you wish to insure the cargo for 130% at the invoice value, the premium for the difference among 130% and 110% should be in your account.
6. For goods sold on CIF basis insurance is to effect by us for 110% of the invoice value against all risks based from warehouse to warehouse clause.
7. The insurance covers only WA and war risks. If extra additional insurance coverage is required, the buyer is borne the extra premium.
8. Please effect insurance in our account of RMB13,200 on the goods against all risks, from Shanghai to Los Angeles.

II. Fill in the blanks.

1. WPA coverage is too narrow for a shipment of this nature, please extend _____ to include TPND.
2. Insurance is to be covered _____ buyers.
3. We note that you wish us to insure shipment to you _____ 10% invoice value.
4. Please insure _____ invoice value _____ 10%.
5. We shall provide such coverage _____ your cost.
6. Our clients request their order to be insured _____ all risks and war risk. Please arrange for the insurance cover accordingly.
7. Please arrange to supply these and charge _____ our account.
8. Regarding insurance, the coverage is _____ 110% of invoice value up to the port of destination only.
9. Buyer's request for insurance coverage up to the inland city can be accepted on condition that such extra premium is for _____ account.
10. Since the premium varies with the extend of _____, extra premium is for buyer's account, should additional risks be _____.
11. The insurance _____ varies with the nature of the goods, the degree of cover desired and the place of destination.

III. Give the English or Chinese equivalents of the followings.

1. 水渍险　　　　_____
2. 保单　　　　　_____
3. 投保人　　　　_____

Chapter 14　Insurance　167

  4. 投保金额　　　　　＿＿＿＿＿＿＿＿＿＿＿＿＿＿＿
  5. 保费　　　　　　　＿＿＿＿＿＿＿＿＿＿＿＿＿＿＿
  6. particular average　＿＿＿＿＿＿＿＿＿＿＿＿＿＿＿
  7. additional coverage　＿＿＿＿＿＿＿＿＿＿＿＿＿＿＿
  8. salvage charges　＿＿＿＿＿＿＿＿＿＿＿＿＿＿＿
  9. underwriter　　　＿＿＿＿＿＿＿＿＿＿＿＿＿＿＿
  10. constructive total loss　＿＿＿＿＿＿＿＿＿＿＿＿＿＿＿

IV. Arrange the following words and phrases in their proper order.

1. which we intend to export we would like you
 all risk over the next three months
 an open cover policy to arrange
 for our chinaware shipment

 ＿＿＿＿＿＿＿＿＿＿＿＿＿＿＿＿＿＿＿＿＿＿＿＿＿＿＿＿＿＿＿＿＿
 ＿＿＿＿＿＿＿＿＿＿＿＿＿＿＿＿＿＿＿＿＿＿＿＿＿＿＿＿＿＿＿＿＿

2. further policies offer us
 on other shipments with you
 if you can we will consider
 competitive rates

 ＿＿＿＿＿＿＿＿＿＿＿＿＿＿＿＿＿＿＿＿＿＿＿＿＿＿＿＿＿＿＿＿＿
 ＿＿＿＿＿＿＿＿＿＿＿＿＿＿＿＿＿＿＿＿＿＿＿＿＿＿＿＿＿＿＿＿＿

3. the shipment for 110% of the invoice value
 if you will arrange as we now desire to have
 on our behalf insured
 against all risks we shall be pleased
 to insure the goods at your end

 ＿＿＿＿＿＿＿＿＿＿＿＿＿＿＿＿＿＿＿＿＿＿＿＿＿＿＿＿＿＿＿＿＿
 ＿＿＿＿＿＿＿＿＿＿＿＿＿＿＿＿＿＿＿＿＿＿＿＿＿＿＿＿＿＿＿＿＿

4. and the insurance policy as required
 with PICC will be sent to you
 we have covered your order through the bank
 together with the other shipping documents

 ＿＿＿＿＿＿＿＿＿＿＿＿＿＿＿＿＿＿＿＿＿＿＿＿＿＿＿＿＿＿＿＿＿
 ＿＿＿＿＿＿＿＿＿＿＿＿＿＿＿＿＿＿＿＿＿＿＿＿＿＿＿＿＿＿＿＿＿

5. of the shipping company's agent   we had
   examined by   opened the case
   in the presence   a local insurance surveyor
   and the contents

   _____
   _____
   _____

V. Translate the following Chinese sentences into English.

1. 请将装运给我们的货物投保水渍险和战争险。

   _____

2. 请按发票价的 110% 投保。

   _____

3. 至于第 345 号合约项下的 300 部相机，我们将自行办理保险。

   _____

4. 至于索赔，我们的保险公司只接受超过实际损失 5% 的部分。

   _____

5. 请告知我们价格是否包括偷窃及提货不着险。

   _____

6. 如果没有你们的明确指示，我们将按一般惯例投保水渍险和战争险。

   _____

7. 很遗憾，我们不能接受这一索赔，因为你们的保险没有包括"破碎险"。

   _____

8. 根据你们常用的 CIF 价格条件，所保的是哪些险别?

   _____

VI. Translation.

> 关于第 ××× 号 3,000 桶铁钉的售货合约，兹通知你方，我们已由中国银行伦敦分行开立了第 ××× 号保兑的、不可撤销的信用证，共计金额 ××× 英镑，有效期至 5 月 15 日。

请注意（做到）上述货物必须在 5 月 15 日前装出，保险必须按发票价的 150% 投保综合险。我们知道，按照一般惯例，你们只按发票价另加 10% 投保，因此额外的保险费用由我们负责。

请按我们的要求办理保险，同时，我们等候你方的装运通知。

VII. Complete the following letters with proper words.

Letter 1

Dear Sir,

Re: Insurance

Answering your _____ of June 25 in _____ to insurance, we would like to _____ you of the following.

All Risks. Generally we cover insurance WPA and war risk in the _____ of definite instructions from our _____. If you desire to _____ all risks, we can provide such coverage at a slightly higher premium.

Breakage. Breakage is a _____ risk, for which an extra _____ will have to be _____. The present rate is about 5%. Claims are payable only for that of the _____, that is over 5%.

Value to be insured. We note that you wish to insure _____ to you for 10% above _____ value, which is having our _____ attention.

We trust the above information will _____ your purpose and _____ your further news.

Yours truly,

Letter 2

Dear Sirs,

We will be _____ a consignment of 100 photocopiers to Daehan Trading Company, Limited, Pusan, Republic of Korea. The consignment is to be _____ on to the S.S. Dashun, which sails from Shanghai on December 16 and is _____ in Pushan on December 19.

Details with _____ to packing and value are _____, and we would be grateful if you could quote a _____ covering all risks from port to port.

As the matter is urgent, we would _____ a prompt reply. Thank you.

Yours truly,

Chapter 15

Complaint and Settlement

> **Lead-in: Case Study**
>
> Fortune Goods has placed an order with Everlong Batteries Ltd. for 12,000 ultra super long-life batteries on May 17. However, after the arrival of the goods, Fortune Goods has found a shortage of the goods, which are 1,200 batteries only. To correct the mistakes, the company lodges a complaint against Everlong Batteries Ltd. and asks them to make up the shortage.

扫描二维码
自学 PPT

1. Complaints

Complaint in international trade is an expression of dissatisfaction with a product or service, either in oral or in writing, from the customer. The party may have a genuine cause for complaint, although some complaints may be made as a result of a misunderstanding or an unreasonable expectation of a product or service. How a customer's complaint is handled will affect the overall level of customer satisfaction and may affect long-term customer loyalty. It is important for providers to have clear procedures for dealing rapidly with any customer complaints, to come to a fair conclusion, and to explain the reasons for what may be perceived by the customer as a negative response.

Usually there are several reasons for complaints: wrong shipment, wrong ordering, wrong destination, shortage, package damage, quality problem, delay in shipment, market claim and others. The purpose of writing a letter of complaint or claim is to get better service or reasonable compensation instead of accusing the others. Accusations do not help either company. They often make it more difficult to correct the errors and to work together in the future. Thus, a complaint letter to a supplier, customer, or other businessperson must be written in a restrained and tactful way. Effective complaint letters should be concise, authoritative, factual, constructive and friendly.

Three elements are usually presented in a complaint or claim letter.

(1) Detailed presentation of facts to explain what is wrong. This explanation should give exact dates, name and quantity of goods, contract number or any other specific information that will make a recheck easier for the reader.

(2) A statement of the inconvenience or loss that has resulted from this error. This strengthens your argument for redress.

(3) A statement of how you want the reader to act. The writer who doesn't know what adjustment is proper should try to stimulate prompt investigation and action.

In general, letters of complaint usually include the following stages.

(1) Background.

(2) Problem, cause and effect.

(3) Solution.

(4) Warning (optional).

(5) Closing.

Sample 1: Complaint on the Shortage of the Goods

July 24, 2016
From: J. Wong
To: Sales Manager
Attn: Mr. David Choi <Everlong Batteries HK@gmail.com>
Re: Order No. 768197

The goods we ordered from your company have not been supplied correctly.

On May 17, 2016, we placed an order with your firm for 12,000 ultra super long-life batteries. The consignment arrived yesterday but contained only 1,200 batteries.

This error put our firm in a difficult position, as we had to make some emergency purchases to fulfill our commitments to all our customers. This caused us considerable inconvenience.

Please make up the shortfall immediately and to ensure that such errors do not happen again. Otherwise, we may have to look elsewhere for our supplies.

I look forward to hearing from you.

Sincerely yours,
J. Wong
Purchasing Officer

Sample 2: Complaint on Wrong Delivery

May 20, 2016 **To:** George **From:** Tony **Re:** Our Order No. BT-6098

Dear George,
    We are writing to complain about the shipment of our Order No. BT-6098 for all-cotton, men's golf shirts of various sizes received this morning. These were ordered on September 13 from the winter catalogue, page 35, and confirmed by telephone and fax on May 15, 2016 (copy enclosed). However, upon unpacking the boxes, we found that they contained 350 women's shirts, all size extra large.
    Since this shipment does not conform to our order and cannot be sold through our golf shops, we cannot accept it as delivered. We do, however, have firm orders for the men's shirts requested. Thus, we suggest that you send someone to pick up the wrongly delivered shirts, and reship the correct order within the next week.
    Thank you for your prompt attention to this matter.
 	
                                                                      Yours faithfully,
                                                                        Tony
                                                                     Chief Buyer

Sample 3: Complain on the Quality of the Sample

August 5, 2016 **To:** Joana **From:** Lily

Dear Joana,
    The samples you sent to us are not what we want. For your better understanding, we airmailed the relevant samples showing you the exact parts which we need for replacement.
    Our customer complained a lot about the poor design and workmanship of the product. Please correct the problems mentioned and provide all parts we need before August 13, or ask someone to bring them here to make the replacement and correction right away.
    Looking forward to your early reply.
 	
                                                                      Sincerely yours,
                                                                      Lily

Sample 4: Complaint on the Quality of the Goods

June 27, 2016
To: Sherlock Ham
From: Fred Johns

We would refer to your consignment of cotton (Order No.120-05), which arrived this morning.

On opening the cases we found that the goods are severely damaged and much inferior in quality to your previous samples.

Please advise us when we can expect to receive our order, as some of our customers have been waiting for up to six weeks.

Please also let us know what we are to do with the cotton now in our possession.

Sincerely yours,
Fred Johns

2. Adjustment to the Complaints

Every complaint or claim, no matter how trivial it seems, is important to the person who makes it. It, therefore, requires a prompt answer or acknowledgment. The answer should be factual, courteous and fair.

If you admit that your company is in error or is willing to take responsibility for the claim, you should write a letter to the customer, expressing apologies and indicating what steps the company is taking to set the matter right.

There are also some times when a customer's request for an adjustment has to be denied. You may not grant the original claim or only agree to partial adjustment. In that case, your letter must be written carefully. The key is not to make the customer feel that he is considered over demanding in making his request, but to assure him that his complaint has been seriously considered and use facts to convince him of your position. Refusal of compensation tests your diplomacy and tact as a writer.

There is no need for the sellers to go into a long story of how the mistake was made. A short explanation may be useful but, generally speaking, the buyers are not interested in hearing how or why the error occurred but only in having the matter put right, in receiving the goods they ordered—or at least value for the money they have paid—or in knowing when they may expect to receive the delayed consignment. Here are some tips for an adjustment letter to a complaint.

(1) Begin with a reference to the date of the original letter of complaint and to the purpose of your letter. If you deny the request, don't state the refusal right away unless you can do so tactfully.

(2) Express your concern over the writer's troubles and your appreciation that he

has written you.

(3) If you deny the request, explain the reasons why the request cannot be granted in as cordial and non-combative manner as possible. If you grant the request, don't sound as if you are doing so in a begrudging way.

(4) If you deny the request, try to offer some partial or substitute compensation or offer some friendly advices.

(5) Conclude the letter cordially, perhaps expressing confidence that you and the writer will continue doing business.

In case the sellers are the first to discover that a mistake has been made, they should not wait for a complaint, but should write, telex or fax at once to let the buyers know, and either put the matter right or offer some compensation.

Sample 1: Reply to the Shortages

July 24, 2016
From: David Choi
Attn: J. Wong
Re: Order No. 2639/L

Dear Mr. Wong,

Please accept our apologies for the error made by our company in fulfilling your order No. 2639/L dated July 23, 2016.

You ordered 12,000 ultra super-long-life premium batteries, but our dispatch office sent 1,200. This was due to a typing error.

The balance of 10,800 batteries was dispatched by express courier to your store this morning and will arrive by August 5, 2016.

Since we value your business, we would like to offer you a 10% discount off for your next order with us.

We look forward to receiving your further orders and assure you that they will be filled correctly.

Yours sincerely,
David Choi
Distributions Manager

Sample 2: Reply to Complaint on Wrong Delivery

May 27, 2016
To: Mr. Smith
From: George

Dear Smith,

Thank you for your letter telling us the shipment of your Order No. BT-6098 for golf shirts. Your complaint was immediately sent to our customer relations representative for investigation.

We have confirmed through our inventory and shipping documents that we have indeed made a mistake on your order. The slip-up occurred in our new, automated inventory control system, which is causing some problems during the data entry stage. Your order number was unfortunately confused with another one (BT-6998), and the error was not caught before the shirts were sent out.

We are very sorry for this mistake and the inconvenience caused you and we want to do everything possible to help you satisfy your customers promptly. We offer to redeliver the correct shirts under BT-6098 by DHL Express Mail upon receiving your directions. As to the non-conforming shirts, please send them back to us, carriage forward.

You are a valued customer and we sincerely regret this mistake. We assure you that we will take every possible action to prevent a repetition of the same mistake in future orders.

Yours sincerely,
George

Sample 3: Reply to the Quality Complaint

August 7, 2016
To: Lily
From: Joana

Dear Lily,

After further conversations regarding the problems you have addressed in the letter of August 5, we have decided as below.

- To save time, we will airmail the parts you need tomorrow.
- Our representative in USA tonight will contact you to make arrangement to go to the job site and correct all problems you have addressed.

We sincerely apologize for the inconvenience and hope all problems will be solved very soon.

Yours sincerely,

Sample 4: Reject the Complaint

June 27, 2016
To: Fred Johns
From: Larry Chen

Dear Johns,

Thank you for your letter of May 15 referring to the consignment of cotton goods sent to you per S.S. Ocean Prince. We regret to note your complaint.

We have investigated the matter thoroughly. As far as we can ascertain, the goods were in first class condition when they left here. The bill of lading is evidence.

It is obvious that the damage you complain of must have taken place during transit. It follows, therefore, that we cannot be held responsible for the damage.

We therefore advise you to make a claim on the shipping company, Prince Line, who should be held responsible.

Thank you for telling us your trouble. If you wish, we would be happy to negotiate with the shipping company on your behalf.

We look forward to resolving this matter as soon as possible.

Yours sincerely,

Sample 5: Refund of the Damaged Goods

April 26, 2016
To: Adeilaide Johnson
From: Nikilesh Ahujha
Sub: Refund of Damaged Goods

Dear Mr. Johnson,

I have just received your letter regarding the shipment of damaged goods you received through Lake Covarde Supplies. I regret for the inconvenience.

According to your claim and details regarding the matter, we have found that your claim of $2,000 for the broken furniture stands legitimate. We have already dispatched the cheque through registered mail at the address provided by you. It will reach at your doorsteps within 2 working days. The damage to your items was caused by a mishap while transporting it. It was an unfortunate accident and a big mistake that the items were not checked before delivery. We take all the responsibility of the damage and are sorry for the inconvenience.

Please keep the damaged items in the same condition in which you received them until our representatives can inspect them. We will inspect the issue within 2 weeks. You will be informed beforehand so that you can provide us the timings which suit you the most.

> I am sure that this unfortunate accident will not hamper our relationship in the future.
>
> Sincerely,
Nikilesh Ahujha

3. Supplementary Information
1) Discrepancy and Claim Clause
In practice, it is strongly recommended that a discrepancy and claim clause be included in a contract. In case the goods delivered are inconsistent with the contract stipulations, the buyer should make a claim against the seller within the validity under the support of a re-inspection certificate or survey report issued by a nominated surveyor.

2) Penalty Clause
A penalty clause sometimes should be included in the contract in case one party fails to implement the contract such as non-delivery, delayed delivery, delayed opening of L/C. Under such clause, the party failing to fulfill the contract must pay a fine, a certain percentage of the total contract value.

3) Points for Attention in Complaining
There are some points for attention in complaining.

(1) For international shipment, any claim by buyer shall reach seller within 21 days after arrival of the goods at the destination stated in B/L accompanied with satisfactory evidence thereof.

(2) For domestic shipment, any claim by buyer shall be posted within 30 days after arrival of the goods at the place of the end user.

(3) Seller shall not be responsible for damages that may result from the use of goods.

(4) Seller shall not be responsible for any amount in excess of the invoice value of the defective goods.

4) Broker
Broker is a person hired to act as an agent or intermediary in making contracts or sales.

5) Underwriter
Underwriter is an agent who underwrites insurance; an employee of an insurance company who determines the acceptability of risks, and the premiums that should be charged.

4. Useful Expressions
(1) *I am writing to inform you that the goods we ordered from your company*

have not been supplied correctly.

(2) I attended your exhibition Sound Systems 2013 at the Fortune Hotel and found it informative and interesting. Unfortunately, my enjoyment of the event was spoiled by a number of organizational problems.

(3) I am a shareholder of Sunshine Bank and I am very concerned regarding recent newspaper reports on the financial situation of the bank. Your company is listed as the auditor in the latest annual report of the bank, so I am writing to you to ask for an explanation of the following issues.

(4) I am writing to inform you of my dissatisfaction with the foods and drinks at the "European Restaurant" on 18 January this year.

(5) On July, 17, we placed an order with your firm for 12,000 ultra super long-life batteries. The consignment arrived yesterday but contained only 1,200 batteries.

(6) Firstly, I had difficulty in registering to attend the event. You set up an on-line registration facility, but I found the facility totally unworkable.

(7) You sent us an invoice for $10,532, but did not deduct our usual 10% discount.

(8) We have found 16 spelling errors and 2 mislabeled diagrams in the sample book.

(9) This error put our firm in a difficult position, as we had to make some emergency purchases to fulfill our commitments to all our customers. This caused us considerable inconvenience.

(10) Even after spending several wasted hours trying to register in this way, the computer would not accept my application.

(11) I am therefore returning the invoice to you for correction.

(12) This large number of errors is unacceptable to our customers, and we are therefore unable to sell these books.

(13) I am writing to ask you to please make up the shortfall immediately and to ensure that such errors do not happen again.

(14) Could I please ask you to look into these matters?

(15) Please send us a corrected invoice for $9,479.

(16) I enclose a copy of the book with the errors highlighted. Please re-print the book and send it to us by next Friday.

(17) Otherwise, we may have to look elsewhere for our supplies.

(18) I'm afraid that if these conditions are not met, we may be forced to take legal action.

(19) If the outstanding fees are not paid by Friday, you will incur a 10% late payment fee.

(20) I look forward to receiving your explanation of these matters.

(21) I look forward to receiving your payment.

(22) I look forward to hearing from you shortly.

(23) We agree that the usual high standards of our products/services were not

met in this instance.

(24) *To prevent re-occurrences we have set up a verification procedure.*

(25) *We assure you that this will not happen again.*

(26) *We have dispatched the new items by express courier. They should arrive by Monday.*

(27) *To show our goodwill, we would like to offer you a 5% discount on your next order with us.*

(28) *We understand how disappointing it can be when your expectations are not met.*

(29) *This is because the guarantee period has expired.*

(30) *This is due to the fact that the guarantee period has expired.*

(31) *If a third party is to blame, direct the complainer to that party.*

(32) *We look forward to receiving your further orders, and assure you that they will be filled correctly/promptly.*

Exercises

I. **Multiple choice.**

1. The goods under contract No. 15408 left here _____.
   A. in a good condition   B. in good conditions
   C. in good condition   D. in the good condition

2. We have lodged a claim _____ ABC&Co. _____ the quality of the goods shipped _____ m.v. Peace.
   A. against, for, by   B. with, for, under
   C. on, against, as per   D. to, for, per

3. As the goods are ready for shipment, we _____ your L/C to be opened immediately.
   A. hope   B. anticipate   C. await   D. expect

4. As arranged, we have effected insurance _____ the goods _____ 110% of the invoice value _____ all risks.
   A. of, at, with   B. for, in, against
   C. on, for, against   D. to, at over

5. It is important that your client _____ the relevant L/C not later than April 15, 2014.
   A. must open   B. has to open   C. open   D. opens

6. The goods _____ shipped already if your L/C had arrived by the end of December.
   A. would be   B. must have been

C. had been　　　　　　　　D. would have been

7. The buyer suggested that the packing of this article _____ improved.
   A. be　　　B. was to be　　C. would be　　D. had to be

8. If we had a sample in hand, we _____ to negotiate business with our end users now.
   A. would be able　　　　　　B. should have
   C. had been able　　　　　　D. should have been able

II. Fill in the blanks.

1. We are lodging a claim _____ the shipment _____ S.S. Red Star _____ short delivery.
2. We hope you will _____ our analysis acceptable.
3. _____ examinations we found that the goods do not agree with the original.
4. Please give our claim your _____ attention and _____ us have your reply _____.
5. We confirm _____ received your remittance _____ $789 _____ settlement _____ our claim.
6. We regret _____ hear that several bags of the last _____ were broken _____ transit.
7. The shipment was _____ by insurance _____ all risks.
8. _____ the time of loading, the goods _____ in good condition.
9. We regret your claim could hardly _____ _____ as the goods were damaged _____ transit.
10. Your claim has been passed on _____ our insurance company, who will get _____ touch _____ you soon.
11. We are very sorry to hear that the goods you received are not _____ _____ the quality expected.
12. Please _____ _____ the matter as one of urgency and let us have your cable reply by the earliest opportunity.

III. Give the English or Chinese equivalents of the followings.

1. 投诉　　　　　_____
2. 客服　　　　　_____
3. 发货不到　　　_____
4. 不可抗力　　　_____
5. 检验报告　　　_____
6. faulty goods　_____

7. replacement _____
8. complete refund _____
9. wrong delivery _____
10. shortage of goods _____

IV. Translate the following Chinese sentences into English.

1. 鉴于原料价格近日上涨，我们不得不调整部分价格。
   _____

2. 很遗憾地通知你方，三号箱及六号箱破损，箱内货物因包装不良严重损坏。
   _____

3. 如果你们退回机器，我们将进行必要的修理，并以最完好的运转情况送还你方。
   _____

4. 对于所遭受的损失，我们不得不要求你方负责。
   _____

5. 无论如何，我们要求你方采取措施以防止类似事件再次发生。
   _____

6. 我们已进行彻底的查询，但所得到的唯一解释是标签混乱了。
   _____

7. 货号有误，导致你方收到错货，我们对此深表歉意。
   _____

8. 请完全按照我们所订的货物立即补发一批。
   _____

V. Complete the following letters with proper words.

Letter 1

Dear Sir,

　　We have received your _____ of 30 May and very much regret that some of your customers are _____ with our serge supplied to your order No. AD-190.

We have been manufacturing serge for many years and can _____ to produce a material that _____ competitor has yet succeeded in producing at the price _____. The reputation _____ by our serge on international markets _____ to their high _____. From what you say it would seem that some of the materials escaped the _____ we normally give to all materials in our _____ department.

We can understand your problem, but regret that we cannot accept your suggestion to take _____ all the _____ serge from the batch about which you _____. Indeed, there should be no need for this, since it is unlikely that the number of _____ serge can be very large. We will of course _____ any piece of serge found not to be _____ and on this particular _____ we are _____ to allow you a special _____ of 5% to _____ for your trouble.

Yours truly,

Letter 2

Dear Sir,

We _____ your consignment of toys this morning. However, on _____ the contents we found that the electric trains _____ on one side of case No. 8 were badly dented, and are unsalable. This case had obviously been dropped, and we _____ this out to your local agents, who _____ the receipt one case side damaged.

No doubt you will take the matter up _____ your insurers; however, for the present, we should be obliged if you would send us 12 replacement trains, Catalogue No. 248T. The _____ report will be forwarded immediately it has been prepared.

Yours sincerely,

Letter 3

Dear Sir,

We have received your fax of 2nd March, and very much _____ the delay in delivering the above. We are now making the necessary _____ for immediate delivery, which means you will have both excavators by 20th March at the latest.

The HERCULES JBM is the most successful excavator we have so far produced. It was an instant success at its first appearance last year at the Hong Kong Building Exhibition and we were soon _____ with orders. Your own order

> was received in November, and according to the waiting list we had then was not _____ for delivery until April. Nevertheless, we put the delivery date _____ so that you would have the machines in March. In February, production was slightly set back by the late arrival of some special parts and this has been _____ for the delay in the present case.
>
> We trust that you will not be unduly inconvenienced _____ having to wait a few more days. The performance of the HERCULES JBM excavators will amply compensate you.
>
> Yours sincerely,

VI. Writing.

Write to your suppliers explaining that in a delivery of metal wastepaper bins twenty-seven were either slightly dented or badly scratched and that you have had to sell them at a price considerably below the recommended retail selling price. Submit a claim for the difference between the recommended retail price and the price at which the damaged bins were actually sold.

Chapter 16

Business Partnership

Lead-in: Case Study

Case One

DDC Clothes Inc. is a well-developed sales organization in USA. It reads about a Chinese company, Charm Textile Export Corporation from the magazine *International Trade*; thus, DDC takes the opportunity to write to Charm Textile Export Corporation, hoping to obtain sales agency business from Charm, to develop market for Charm's textiles in America.

Case Two

Shenzhen Citex Electronics Technology Co., Ltd. advertises on alibaba.com, looking for distributors in Europe and America to distribute their electronic products. Vi & Kee Co., Ltd is writing a letter, with the hope of obtaining the opportunity to be such a role.

Case Three

Syfaa Textiles Trading Inc. is expecting to be granted franchise license from a famous brand garments company. The market manager of Syfaa searches the Internet and finds the relative information and then writes a letter, introducing Syfaa, expressing the intention of being franchisee.

Case Four

Wal-Mart Stores Inc. makes an advertisement for a company to open another chain store in South Africa. Good Neighbor Inc. reads the information and is very interested in it. It sends a letter to Wal-Mart Stores Inc., describing itself as the most relevant promotional and distribution channel.

扫描二维码
自学 PPT

1. Agency

A vast amount of international trade is handled not by direct negotiation between importer and exporter but by agencies. Internationally, agency can simply indicate such a relation that the exporter empowers a foreign businessman to conduct business performance abroad. An international trade agent acts as a representative for companies that want to do business in other countries. Such agents can facilitate every step of the deal, from locating a supplier to verifying shipment. This type of agent has representatives and offices in many foreign countries and is familiar with the pertinent laws, including trade restrictions, tariffs, and so forth. Working with an international trade agent may allow a company to avoid some common trading pitfalls.

Agency is a common practice in the international trade, especially in marketing, transportation, insurance and advertisement, etc. According to the degree of authority that the agents were invested, they could always be classified into three types: general agent, sole agent and commission agent.

There are mainly four steps in writing an application letter of being an agent.

(1) Briefly describe the source of information through which you got to know that they want an agent.

(2) State your experience of being any kind of agent and introduce yourself or your company as well as the marketing plan.

(3) Show your interest in acting as an agent and provide some related companies for them to refer to.

(4) List some general terms for them to consider if you want to and then express your eager willingness as a closing.

Sample 1: Importer Offering Sole Agency Service

February 17, 2016
To: Catherine Wang
From: Lester Bemstein

Dear Mrs. Wang,

We have a well-developed sales organization in USA and are represented by a large staff in various parts of the country. From their reports, it seems clear that there is a good demand for your textiles and as we believe you are not directly represented in USA, we are writing to offer our service as your sole agent.

Considering the wide connections which we are fortunate enough to possess, we think you will agree that a 5% commission on net sales is quite reasonable. We are also prepared to guarantee payment of all accounts, for which we should require a commission of 2.5%.

You will naturally wish to have information about us. We refer you to the CITI Bank who is consented to answer your inquiries as to our financial standing and so on.

We're looking forward to your favorable reply.

Yours sincerely,
Lester Bemstein
Overseas Sales Director

Sample 2: Declining a Request to Be the Sole Agent

February 27, 2016
To: Lester Bemstein
From: Catherine Wang

Dear Mr. Bemstein,

Thank you for your inquiry regarding the sole agency for the sale of our textile products in USA.

After serious consideration, we think that it would be premature to commit ourselves at this stage when the record of transactions shows only a moderate volume of business.

Please do not misinterpret the above remark, which in no way implies dissatisfaction. As a matter of fact, we are quite satisfied with the amount of business you have brought us. However, we are of the opinion that a bigger turnover must be reached to justify establishing the agency.

In view of the above, we think it advisable to postpone this matter until your future sales warrant such a step. We hope that you will agree with us on this point and continue to give us your cooperation.

Yours faithfully,
Catherine Wang

Sample 3: Entrusting Customer with Sole Agent

February 27, 2016
To: Lester Bemstein
From: Catherine Wang

Dear Mr. Bemstein,

We have received your letter of February 17, and, after careful consideration, have decided to entrust you with the sole agency for our textile products in USA.

The agency agreement has been drawn up for the duration of 1 year, automatically renewable on expiration for a similar period unless notice is given to the contrary; the terms and conditions are set forth in details.

Enclosed is a copy of the draft. Please go over the provisions and advise us whether they meet with your approval.

We shall do all our power to assist you in establishing a mutually beneficial trade.

Sincerely yours,
Catherine Wang
Manager
Export Department

2. Distribution

Distribution is the process of making a product or service available for a consumer or business user, using direct means, or using indirect means with intermediaries.

Distribution of products takes place by means of channels. Channels are sets of interdependent organizations (called intermediaries) involved in making the product available for consumption. Merchants are intermediaries that buy and resell products. Agents and brokers are intermediaries that act on behalf of the producer but do not take title to the products.

Distributor is an entity that buys noncompeting products or product lines, warehouses them, and resells them to retailers or directly to the end users or customers. Most distributors provide strong manpower and cash support to the supplier or manufacturer's promotional efforts. They usually also provide a range of services (such as product information, estimates, technical support, after-sales services, credit) to their customers.

No matter how wonderful a product is, it can't benefit your business if you don't own the rights to sell it. Items that are patented copyrighted or trademarked have a limited distribution, and you won't be able to sell or otherwise distribute them in your business without getting permission from the person or entity that owns the rights, and that is not always the manufacturer. A well-written business letter can be your first step toward getting distribution rights to the product.

Sample 1: Manufacturer Looking for Distributors

April 7, 2016
To: Lester Bemstein
From: Lukas Feng

Dear Mr. Bemstein,

We are Shangduo Leather Goods Co., Ltd., established in 1999 in Guangzhou, China, specializing in all kinds of customized leather premiums, unique leather accessories, corporate leather gifts, office/hotel supplies and more, with floor space of more than 10,000 square meters, more than 400 employees and 3 production lines. With so many years of development, we now have had 2 branch companies, one in Beijing and the other in Shanghai.

Our products are receiving warm welcome, and we are expanding our business into North America, expecting a reliable Canadian or American organization to be our distributor. If you are interested, we can contact further for the matters concerning the distribution contract.

> For more information, please reach us by shangduo@163.com, or visit our website: http://www.shangduo.com. We are looking forward to your early reply.
>
> Sincerely yours,

Sample 2: Asking for Distribution Right

> **To:** Lukas Feng
> **From:** Lester Bemstein
> **Date:** April 12, 2016
> **Subject:** Establishing Distribution Relationship

> Dear Sirs,
>
>   We understand from your online message released on April 7 that you are seeking a distributor for the range of your leather products. We have been a distributor for years, dealing with leather products for 12 years, and have wide connections in this area.
>
>   Also, market statistics show that the demand for goods of this line has increased in recent years at our end, and we believe that there is a profitable market waiting to be developed.
>
>   We've attached our details, including our business and financial status. If we can meet your requirements, could you please forward catalogue and pricing information? We are glad to enter into distributor contract with you.
>
>   We look forward to receiving your early reply and assure you of a mutually beneficial cooperation between us.
>
> Yours sincerely,
Lester Bemstein
Sales Director

Sample 3: Reply to Accept the Requirement for Distribution Right

> **To:** Lester Bemstein
> **From:** Lukas Feng
> **Date:** April 15, 2016
> **Re:** Establishing Distribution Relationship

> Dear Lester Bemstein,
>
>   Thank you very much for your letter of April 12, expressing your interest in distribution-ship with us. After immediate and overall consideration, we accept you being our exclusive distributor in Canada on the understanding that you countersign the contract attached. Of course, we can come to further discussion, if there is anything that can't be agreed upon.

We are attaching our catalogue and price list for your information, and also some samples are airmailed to you at no charge.

If you have any question, please contact us at 001-780-329-6279. We're looking forward to receiving early countersigned contract.

Yours sincerely,
Lukas Feng
General Manager

Sample 4: Informing Distributor

From: Mr. Wilson
To: Mr. Jackson

Dear Mr. Jackson,

I am writing to inform you that recently we have extended our distributorship in your city, Oak Park.

We have authorized "Wayne Chemists" as our local distributor in Oak Park. They will be selling our products. They have many stores in Illinois and we are expanding our business through them. They also have proper arrangements or marketing and it will benefit us.

So, please approach them for our products for your business needs. You can contact us if you need any other information about them.

Contact details of our distributor:
Wayne Chemists
152, Miguel's Place
Luis St, Oak Park-41253

Sincerely yours,
Mr. Wilson
Sales Manager
Ferguson Pharmaceuticals

3. Franchise

The franchise is a license to operate an individually owned business as though it were part of a chain of outlets or stores. Usually, there are three types of business concepts using the franchise model.

(1) Distributorship, such as a car dealership.

(2) Brand name licensing. Sports franchises fall into this category.

(3) Business format, where a franchisee purchases the right to operate a unique

扫描二维码
浏览视频
"What Is a Partnership"

business system.

Some of these ventures are difficult to launch because of the costs, whereas others are more easily attained.

Sample 1: Asking for Franchise License

To: Cathy
From: Annie Huang
Subject: Establishing Franchise Relationship

Dear Cathy,

From the Chamber of Commerce in America, we have learned that you are an American fast food restaurant franchisor and have been supplying the best quality fast food all over the world, and we are sure there is a large demand for various exotic fast foods in our city. We hope to obtain franchising right from you.

We are Shanghai Simenki Restaurant Co., Ltd, one of the largest fast food restaurants in China, with more than 40 chain restaurants in all major cities. We have been dealing with a large variety of foods from Italy and USA, and consider that we have considerable experience in this field. If we can meet your standard, we are glad to enter into a franchise agreement with you.

A bright prospect for your products in our market is foreseeable. We look forward to receiving your favorable reply and assure you of our best achievements at all times.

Yours sincerely,
Annie Huang
Ferguson Pharmaceuticals

Sample 2: Reply to Grant the Franchise License

To: Annie Huang
From: Cathy
Re: Establishing Franchise Relationship

Dear Annie Huang,

Thank you very much for your letter of May 20, showing your interest in our business. After thorough consideration, we accept your requirement to be one of our franchisees in your territory on condition that you can meet the basic requirements in the FDD we are attaching here.

As you've read about, we are one of the fastest growing franchises and the largest single-brand restaurant chain and the largest restaurant operator in the world, with 40,855 restaurants in 105 countries and territories. Our subway's menu varies between countries, most significantly in places where there are religious requirements relating to the meats served.

Please refer to the attachment for our catalogue and company profile. Your latest details, especially the banker's reference showing your net worth and your liquid assets, are highly appreciated, which will be an essential factor for further consideration to enter into the franchise agreement.

With various franchise opportunities available, we will help you make the right decisions so you can hit the ground running and grow your business, quickly and easily. If you have any question, please do not hesitate to contact us at 1-860-270-8689. We're looking forward to your early reply.

Yours sincerely,
Cathy
Market Manager

Sample 3: Reply to Decline the Franchise License

To: Annie Huang
From: Cathy
Re: Establishing Franchise Relationship

Dear Annie Huang,

Thank you very much for your letter of May 20. As you know, we primarily sell submarine sandwiches (subs) and salads as well as breakfast sandwiches, English muffins and flatbreads, which we can't be sure whether there is a ready market in your territory.

I regret to say that, at this stage, an arrangement to grant you franchise would be rather premature. We would, however, be willing to be engaged in trial cooperation with your company to see how the arrangement works. It would be necessary for you to test the market for our products at your end.

Please click the attachment to get our menu and our company profile for your reference and our representative will be sent to your market soon to discuss details concerning the trial business.

If you have any question, please do not hesitate to contact us at 1-860-270-8689. We're looking forward to your early reply.

Yours sincerely,
Cathy
Market Manager

4. Chain Store

Chain stores are retail outlets that share a brand and central management, and usually have standardized business methods and practices. The store must have more than 10 units under the same brand and have a central headquarters, otherwise it offers franchise contracts or is publicly traded. These characteristics also apply to chain restaurants and some service-oriented chain businesses. In retail, dining, and many service categories, chain businesses have come to dominate the market in many parts of the world.

Chain stores are usually a group of retail outlets owned by one firm and spread nationwide or worldwide, such as Body Shop, K-Mart, Wal-Mart. Chain stores, usually have similar architecture, store design and layout, and choice of products.

Sample 1: Applying to Join in Chain Store Business

Date: January 13, 2016
To: Mr.Karl
From: Hu Yuheng
Subject: Chain Store Business

Dear Mr. Karl,

Through your online message, we have learned with pleasure that you are granting the chain store business. We are writing to apply for such right.

We are a leading trade company, specializing in grocery stores, which, we think, falls within your business line. We have very large numbers of permanent customers in our 36 chain stores in China, and considerable sales volume.

Attached is our profile and detailed information about our business.

We are looking forward to your favorable reply early.

Sincerely yours,
Hu Yuheng
Import Department

Sample 2: Accepting to Join the Chain Store Business

Date: January 19, 2016
To: Hu Yuheng
From: Mr.Karl
Re: Your Application for Chain Store Business

Dear Mr. Hu,

We are pleased to receive your letter of January 13, applying for being granted chain store business permission. We are writing to offer you such right.

From the material attached, we find that you are handling in grocery stores, and have 36 chain stores in your country, which is really of interest to us.

As you may have acknowledged, we, the Kroger Co., a supermarket retail chain, have owned over 2,400 supermarkets all over the United States. We are implementing a new marketing strategy and expanding our business globally.

> We are sending you, under separate cover, our proposal, terms and conditions for cooperation.
>
> For any problem or further information, please do not hesitate to contact us at 1-866-221-4141. Your early reply will be appreciated.
>
> Sincerely yours,
Karl Black
Market Manager

Sample 3: Refusing to Join the Chain Store Business

> **Date:** January 19, 2016
> **To:** Hu Yuheng
> **From:** Mr.Karl
> **Re:** Your Application for Chain Store Business

> Dear Mr. Hu,
>
> Thank you very much for your letter of January 13, expressing your interest in our chain store business. As described on our website, we own jewellery stores, hypermarkets, convenience stores and department stores all over the United States. And today, we rank as one of the world's largest retailers.
>
> However, after thorough consideration, we regret to say that, in view of sales volume, a company headquartered in Shanghai or Beijing will be appreciated to being granted chain store business.
>
> Since this is our first step into the Chinese market, we should take turnover into the foremost consideration. Please recommend chain stores in the cities mentioned above.
>
> Thank you again for your kind consideration and favor to us.
>
> Yours sincerely,
Karl Black
Market Manager

5. Supplementary Information
1) Agent

An agent arises when one person authorizes another person to make contracts on his behalf with third parties. It follows that there will usually be an actual appointment to confer the necessary authority on the agent. Once appointed, he shall act for the principal within the agreed authority to make contracts on the principal's behalf.

According to the degree of authority that the agents were invested, agents are classified into three basic types: general agent, ordinary agent, and exclusive agent.

(1) A general agent, a firm or a person, is appointed by the principal to transact all business of a specific kind in a specific place on behalf of the principal for some rate of commission during a specific period of time under the general agreement or contract.

(2) An ordinary agent is appointed by the principal to carry out certain activities on behalf of the principal within a specific area for a specific period. A principal may appoint several ordinary agents in one area under the ordinary agreement or contract.

(3) An exclusive agent is the only one that is authorized by the principal to exclusively transact the business of his principal of a specific kind within a specific period of time under the exclusive agreement or contract.

2) Intermediary

An intermediary (or go-between) is a third party that offers intermediation services between two trading parties. The intermediary acts as a conduit for goods or services offered by a supplier to a consumer. Typically the intermediary offers some added value to the transaction that may not be possible by direct trading.

3) Franchise

Franchise is a license to operate an individually owned business as though it were part of a chain of outlets or stores. It concerns businesses that use a franchise model. Some of these ventures are difficult to launch because of the costs, whereas others are more easily attained.

4) Distributorship

It means to grant the right to sell the parent company's products such as car dealership or vending machine routes.

5) Brand Name Licensing

This gives the licensee the right to use the parent company's brand in conjunction with the operation of their own business. Here, the product or service is franchised (or licensed) and not the business itself. For example, a sports store in a small town is granted the exclusive rights in that town to sell Nike's products. Sports franchises fall into this category as well.

6) Business Format

It is the most common franchise format where a franchisee purchases the right to operate a unique business system that has an established history and track record created by the franchisor. In exchange for a pre-determined royalty structure, the franchisor provides initial and ongoing training, sales and marketing support, and many other services and assistance to aid in the franchisee's business success.

7) Financial Status

Financial status, also referred to as financial standing or financial condition, is the status of the assets, liabilities, and owners' equity of an organization or a person, as reflected in its financial statements. It is mostly used to determine borrowing qualification.

8) Franchising Royalties

Franchising royalties are fees that franchisees pay to the franchiser in exchange for the existing structure and brand rather than incurring the expense and time of structuring and creating a business model independently. Franchising royalties can vary from a monthly percentage of profits to an annual profit split to a monthly flat rate, depending upon the stipulations of the franchise agreement. Franchising royalties are usually used to support the overhead of the franchise operation itself. Frequently, royalties are paid by a percentage of monthly profits for the life of the franchise agreement, and are non-negotiable.

9) FDD

FDD (franchise disclosure document) is a legal document which is presented to prospective buyers of franchises in the pre-sale disclosure process in the United States. It was originally known as the Uniform Franchise Offering Circular (UFOC), prior to revisions made by the Federal Trade Commission in July 2007.

10) Bank Reference

Bank reference, also known as banker's reference, is information released by a bank about a customer, to another bank or lending institution. Bank references generally include: number of years of a customer's relationship with the bank; number of loans and the amounts of their balances; type and quality of collaterals; a copy of the customer's latest statement of financial affairs on file with the bank.

Banks usually are under no obligation to seek the customer's approval (or to reveal the identity of the recipient) for releasing such information.

11) To Customize

To customize means producing, manufacturing or modifying something according to a customer's individual or special requirements.

12) Retail Outlet

A retail outlet is a store that simply sells merchandise purchased by the store from a wholesaler, or manufactured by the company that owns the store directly to the consumer, or a store that is opened by the manufacturer, often near the factory, for the purposes of selling over-produced or irregular merchandise at discount prices. Some retail outlets, generally in a fixed location, are large stores with a wide variety of merchandise, while others are small specialty boutiques.

6. Useful Expressions

(1) *We have many connections in your country.*

(2) *He set up in business and soon had a good connection.*

(3) *We have received a number of enquires from our trade connections here for your bicycles.*

(4) *We have established a business connection with them.*

(5) *Please let us know whether you now represent any other suppliers in the same line.*

(6) *We ask if you wish to be represented in this market.*

(7) *In view of the fact that the rate of premium you quoted is quite reasonable, we have decided to entrust your company with the insurance of this shipment.*

(8) *The local bank issues a trust deed for payment, then sends it to a correspondent bank at the seller's end by means of mail and entrusts him to pay the money to the sellers.*

(9) *We have entrusted this matter to our representative, who will have a discussion with you.*

(10) *They appointed him as general manager of the new company.*

(11) *Mr. Smith was appointed to be the sole agent for the sale of our product in your market.*

(12) *Regarding the sale of Hisense color TV sets in the European market, we have appointed ABC Co. as our agent.*

(13) *If you were to appoint us as your agent, we should be prepared to discuss the rate of commission with you.*

(14) *Our business covers a wide range of light industrial products.*

(15) *We can supply woolen blankets in a wide range of designs.*

(16) *We are sending you a full range of samples.*

(17) *The above price includes your commission of 2%.*

(18) *We do not pay any commission on our traditional products.*

(19) *Considering your sustained efforts to cooperate with us, we agree to raise your commission to 3%.*

(20) *For large sales volume, we can grant you a commission of 5%.*

(21) *We can grant you a commission of 5% on large sales volume.*

Exercises

I. **Choose the appropriate word or words to complete the sentences.**

1. Considering your sustained efforts to cooperate (between, with, to) us, we agree to raise your commission to 3%.
2. We have entrusted this matter (to, for, with) our distributor, who will have a discussion with you for an acceptable resolution.
3. We have received a number of enquires from our trade connections for your bicycles, and we are confident to achieve the sales (amount, figure, turnover) requirement for a sole agent.

4. The demand for fast food has increased in recent years in our area and we believe that there is a profitable market of such chain restaurant waiting to be (occupied, developed, opened).
5. Regarding the sale of Hisense color TV sets in the European market, we have appointed ABC Co. (for, as, become) our agent.
6. We have very large numbers of permanent customers in our 30 chain stores in China, with (considerable, considerate, considering) sales volume.
7. If you were to appoint us as your agent, we should be prepared to discuss the (amount, rate, figure) of commission.
8. I've got your business information online and learned that you are applying for a franchise business. Please refer to the attachments for our franchise agreement. Maybe we can come (into, for, to) terms.
9. We currently have the sole agency for another computer company. Under the terms of the contract, we are barred (from, against, for) selling any other company's products.
10. Having had experience in dealing with similar products, we have wide (connections, relationship, ways) in this market and a number of long-standing customers.

II. **Arrange the following words and phrases in their proper order.**

1. 10 per cent on orders placed   as
    would be heavy,   during the first 12 months
    we feel that   would be a reasonable figure
    the early work on development   however

    _____
    _____

2. the best quality fast food   fast food restaurant franchise
    to find that   and have been supplying
    from the online message   we are pleased
    an America   you are

    _____
    _____

3. due to   a profitable market
    the increasing demand   and
    we are reforming   expanding into Europe
    for goods of this line   at our end
    in recent years   our marketing strategies
    there is   we believe

4. the grant for   immediate and overall consideration
   a sole agency   a much larger turnover
   I regret   you
   after   should first meet
   so   at this stage
   to say that   would have
   to build up   the sales volume requirement

5. should be offered   the wide connections
   in view of   your sales figure
   on net sales   to meet
   on the condition that   we possess
   a 5% commission   we are confident

III. **Fill in the blanks.**

1. From your _____ message, we understand that you are seeking a distributor for _____ your leather products.
2. We are a leading trade company, specializing in grocery stores, which, we think, _____ your business line.
3. We have a well-developed sales organization in USA and are _____ by a large staff in various parts of the country.
4. Enclosed is a copy of the agreement. Please go over _____ and advise us whether they meet with your approval.
5. We would, however, be willing to _____ trial cooperation with your company to see how the arrangement works.
6. We look forward to receiving your _____ and assure you of our best achievements at all times.
7. In view of _____ we possess, we think you will agree that a 5% commission on net sales is quite reasonable.
8. If it is of your interest, we can _____ further contact for the matters concerning distribution contract.

9. After serious consideration, we think that it would be _____ to commit ourselves at this stage.
10. Your latest details are highly appreciated, which will be an essential factor for further consideration to _____ the franchise agreement.
11. We have been a distributor for years, _____ leather products for 12 years, and have wide connections in this area.
12. We are _____ our business _____ North America, expecting a reliable Canadian or American organization to be our distributor.

IV. **Give the English or Chinese equivalents of the followings.**

1. 现金流 _____
2. 营业额 _____
3. 独家代理商 _____
4. 净销售额 _____
5. 经销商 _____
6. 零售商 _____
7. 代理佣金 _____
8. 门店 _____
9. 启动成本 _____
10. 销售量 _____
11. after-sales services _____
12. franchise royalty _____
13. customized leather premiums _____
14. banker's reference _____
15. the terms and conditions _____
16. a mutually beneficial trade _____
17. business format _____
18. agent's territory _____
19. wide connections _____
20. liquid assets _____

V. **Complete the following letters with proper words.**

Letter 1

Dear Anson,

    Thank you very much for your kind _____ for distribution ship with us. As required in your last letter, I'd like to _____ you some items in South Africa for your easy _____ first. The details are as attached. We are also inviting you to visit our _____ at www.shvfurniture.com to know more about us.

Regarding the _____ contract, normally we only accept terms and conditions based on exclusive distributor agreement. In view of our wide _____ popular and competitive products, we are sure you can make sales at your end easily. If needed, some free _____ can be airmailed to you for further _____.

We would also like to get some _____ information concerning your sales figure and your _____ standing, which can help us to _____ some agreements and facilitate our cooperation.

We are looking forward to the mutually beneficial _____ between us.

Best regards,
John

Letter 2

Dear Sirs,

We would like to offer our services as agents for the _____ of your products in Australia.

As agents of the highest standing, our company was _____ in 1926. We have been agents in several West European countries.

There is a growing _____ in Australia for Chinese textiles, especially for fancy worsted suiting, printed cotton and nylon fabrics. There are great prospects for good quality fabrics at _____ prices, and according to a recent chamber of commerce survey, the demand for Chinese textiles is likely to grow _____ during the next 2 or 3 years.

If you would send us details of your _____, with samples and prices, we could inform you of their _____ for the Australian market, and also indicate the patterns and _____ for which sales are likely to be _____. We would then arrange to call on our customers for your collection.

You will naturally wish to have _____ and may write to Barclays Bank Ltd., 99 Piccadilly, Manchester, or to any of our _____, whose names we will be glad to send you.

We feel sure we should have no difficulty in arranging _____ to suit us both. We are looking forward to hearing from you soon.

Yours faithfully,
Cedric Jones

VI. Translation.

> Dear Sirs,
>
> Statistics from Canadian Cosmetics, Toiletry and Fragrance Association show a marked increasing demand for cosmetics toiletries in Canada in recent years. So, we are convinced that there is a considerable market here for your products.
>
> There is every sign that an advertising campaign, even on a modest scale, would produce very good results if it were backed by an efficient system of distribution.
>
> We are well-known distributors of over 15 years' standing, with branches in most of the principal cities in Canada. With knowledge of the local conditions, we feel we have the experience and the resources necessary to bring about a market development of your trade in this country. Reference to the Canadian Cosmetics, Toiletry and Fragrance Association and the Canadian Chamber of Commerce would enable you to verify our statement.
>
> If you were to appoint us as your distributor, we should be prepared to discuss the terms and conditions of the contract.
>
> We hope you will see a worthwhile opportunity in our proposal, and that we may look forward to your early decision.
>
> Yours faithfully,

Part 4

Simulation Training in Business Writing

Chapter 17

Business Correspondence

1. Business Transaction

Case 1

Ms. Joanne Zhang, sales manager of Poseidon Trading Co., Ltd., sourced the following information.

Company name: Roslyns Emporium

About us: We are selling gifts in the UK, but want to buy ladies fashion, jewelry, handbags, gifts, greeting cards, etc. from other countries.

Contact person: Ms. Roslyn Calder, Overseas Department Manager

Telephone: 44-01651-851260

Address: 3 Pringle Avenue, Tarves, Aberdeenshire, United Kingdom

Website: http://www.RoslynsEmporium.co.uk

The followings are details of Joanne Zhang's company.

Company name: Poseidon Trading Co., Ltd.

Main markets: South America, Asia and USA

Product: 100% handmade EMB camisole, 100% handmade beads emb slim bag, 100% handmade beads EMB handbag, 100% handmade beads EMB top

Contact person: Ms. Joanne Zhang, Sales Manager

Telephone: 86-755-88261899

Fax: 86-755-88261880

Address: 4/F, Bonham Centre, 79-85 Bonham Strand East, Sheung Wan, Hong Kong

Website: public.fotki.com/Handbag/

Step 1

Joanne logs on the website of this company and finds it is reliable, so she writes a letter of inquiry to Roslyn.

Chapter 17 Business Correspondence

To: "Ms. Roslyn Calder" <RoslynCalder@RoslynsEmporium.com>
From: "Ms. Joanne Zhang" <PoseidonTrading@hotmail.com>
Date: January 10, 2016
Subject: Establishing Business Relationship

Step 2
Roslyn Calder replies immediately after receiving the letter.

To: "Ms. Joanne Zhang" <PoseidonTrading@hotmail.com>
From: "Ms. Roslyn Calder" <RoslynCalder@RoslynsEmporium.com>
Date: January 11, 2016
Subject: Establishing Business Relationship

Dear Joanne,

   Thank you for your letter of January 10. We are glad to enter into business relations with you.

   As you know, we have been specializing in gifts in the UK for years, and are interested in ladies fashion, jewelry, handbags, gifts, greeting cards, etc. from other countries.

We are currently interested in your 100% handmade beads emb slim bag and 100% handmade beads EMB handbag. price list and your illustrated catalogue will be greatly appreciated.

We are looking forward to your early reply.

Sincerely yours,
Roslyn Calder
Overseas Department Manager

Step 3

Upon getting the reply from Roslyn, Joanne sends an E-mail back immediately.

To: " Ms. Roslyn Calder "< RoslynCalder@RoslynsEmporium.com >
From: "Ms. Joanne Zhang"< PoseidonTrading@hotmail.com >
Date: January 11, 2016
Subject: Price List and Catalogues

Step 4

Roslyn thinks the prices are a little higher than expected, so she replies, asking for 10% less than the original ones and FOB price rather than CIF price. She says prices for beads EMB bags are dropping in international market. She hopes to get delivery within one month after order confirmed.

To: "Ms. Joanne Zhang"< PoseidonTrading@hotmail.com >
From: " Ms. Roslyn Calder "< RoslynCalder@RoslynsEmporium.com>
Date: January 12, 2016
Subject: Price Term

Dear Joanne,

Thanks for the offer attached in your last E-mail. We appreciate the good quality of your goods, unfortunately, we are not ready to accept the offer on your terms. Your price appears to be on rather high side. Actually we can obtain the products with similar quality through another channel at a much lower price than you quoted us.

As you know, the market for beads EMB bags is declining.

Would you please make some allowance, say 10% on your quoted price, which would help to push the sales of your goods in our markets. If you can do so, we will possibly make regular orders from you. We hope you will take advantage of this chance so that both of us will benefit from the expanding market.

We will appreciate it very much if you will consider our counter offer favorably and fax us your acceptance as soon as possible.

We can only do business on FOB basis, and would like you to convert your CIF price into FOB price. In addition, we hope to get delivery within one month after order confirmed.

Sincerely yours,
Roslyn

Step 5

Joanne sends an E-mail back immediately.

To: "Ms. Roslyn Calder"< RoslynCalder@RoslynsEmporium.com>
From: "Ms. Joanne Zhang"< PoseidonTrading@hotmail.com >
Date: January 13, 2016
Subject: Price Term

Step 6

Roslyn accepts Joanne's offer and places an order. She also refers to the shipment and terms of payment.

To: "Ms. Joanne Zhang"< PoseidonTrading@hotmail.com >
From: "Ms. Roslyn Calder"< RoslynCalder@RoslynsEmporium.com>
Date: January 14, 2016
Subject: Order No. JB369 for Handmade Beads EMB Bags

Dear Joanne,

Thank you for your quotation of January 13. We are glad to place an order with you for the captioned goods on the terms and conditions as below:

Article: 100% handmade beads EMB slim bag and handbag

Item No.	Quantity (bag)	Unit Price (USD)
SB356	150	8.5
SB357	100	10
SB358	120	11
HB202	130	12
HB203	100	13
HB204	150	15
HB205	100	16

> **Payment:** payable by irrevocable confirmed sight L/C on FOB Hong Kong
> **Shipment:** before February 29
> **Packing:** each in an air bubble plastic bag, 10 bags in a box and 50 boxes in a carton
>
> Since this is the first order, we will pay special attention to the quality.
>
> Looking forward to receiving our order early.
>
> Sincerely yours,
> Roslyn

Step 7

Joanne acknowledges acceptance of the order and promises to fulfill the order as required. She reminds Roslyn of the opening of the L/C timely.

> **To:** "Ms. Roslyn Calder"< RoslynCalder@RoslynsEmporium.com>
> **From:** "Ms. Joanne Zhang"< PoseidonTrading@hotmail.com >
> **Date:** January 16, 2016
> **Subject:** Order No. JB369

Step 8

Roslyn opens the L/C and sends details to Joanne.

To: "Ms. Joanne Zhang"< PoseidonTrading@hotmail.com >
From: "Ms. Roslyn Calder"< RoslynCalder@RoslynsEmporium.com>
Date: January 19, 2016
Subject: Opening L/C

Dear Joanne,

We are pleased to tell you that we have opened L/C No.116369 for USD10,350 under our order No. JB369 on CIF basis on January 18 through "Bank of China, London Branch" to your bank.

Please check the L/C and confirm us by cable.

Sincerely yours,
Roslyn

Step 9

Joanne reads the E-mail and finds some discrepancies in the L/C: the total amount should be USD10,305 instead of USD10,350, price terms FOB instead of CIF. Joanne sends Roslyn an E-mail immediately, asking her to amend the L/C soon.

To: "Ms. Roslyn Calder"< RoslynCalder@RoslynsEmporium.com>
From: "Ms. Joanne Zhang"< PoseidonTrading@hotmail.com >
Date: January 20, 2016
Subject: L/C Amendment

Step 10

Roslyn makes an amendment of the L/C, feeling very sorry for her carelessness.

To: "Ms. Joanne Zhang"< PoseidonTrading@hotmail.com >
From: "Ms. Roslyn Calder"< RoslynCalder@RoslynsEmporium.com>
Date: January 21, 2016
Subject: L/C Amendment

Dear Joanne,

 We are so sorry to learn from your last letter that there are some discrepancies in the L/C No. 116369.

 We have made the relevant amendments as required and to save time, we have cabled the amended L/C to you. Please check it and confirm by fax.

 Thank you for your consideration and we apologize for the inconvenience and trouble caused.

Sincerely yours,
Roslyn

Step 11

Joanne receives the correctly amended L/C, and ships the goods. Then she dispatches shipping documents immediately and asks for payment.

To: "Ms. Roslyn Calder"< RoslynCalder@RoslynsEmporium.com>
From: "Ms. Joanne Zhang"< PoseidonTrading@hotmail.com>
Date: February 2, 2016
Subject: Asking for Payment

Step 12

Roslyn receives the goods, but finds a mistake of the number ordered for, Article No. SB356 is 100 instead of 150 and Article No. SB357 is 150 instead of 100.

To: "Ms. Joanne Zhang"< PoseidonTrading@hotmail.com >   **From:** "Ms. Roslyn Calder"< RoslynCalder@RoslynsEmporium.com >   **Date:** March 16, 2016   **Subject:** Wrong Delivery of Order No.JB369
Dear Joanne, 　　We are pleased to tell you that the handmade EMB bags under our order No. JB369 have arrived. However, on unpacking the boxes, we found serious mistakes in the number of Article No.SB356 and Article No.SB357. For your detailed information, we attach a copy of our order and the packing list. 　　Please solve the problem soon, instructing us how we should deal with the surplus in our hands currently.   　　　　　　　　　　　　　　　　　　　　　　　　　　　Sincerely yours, 　　　　　　　　　　　　　　　　　　　　　　　　　　　Roslyn

Step 13

Receiving Roslyn's E-mail, Joanne replies immediately, explaining the reason for the mistake: a new employee caused the error when the order was outbound. Joanne also provides ways to solve the problem.

To: "Ms. Roslyn Calder"< RoslynCalder@RoslynsEmporium.com >   **From:** "Ms. Joanne Zhang"< PoseidonTrading@hotmail.com >   **Date:** March 17, 2014   **Subject:** Complaint Settlement

Step 14

Receiving Joanne's E-mail, Roslyn replies to accept the additional 50 bags of Article No. SB357 for a 10% discount but cancel the 50 bags of Article No. SB356.

To: "Ms. Joanne Zhang"< PoseidonTrading@hotmail.com >
From: "Ms. Roslyn Calder"< RoslynCalder@RoslynsEmporium.com>
Date: March 21, 2016
Subject: Settlement of Order No. JB369

Dear Joanne,

    Thanks for your last E-mail. After careful consideration, we have made a decision to accept the additional 50 bags of Article No. SB357 for a 10% discount. However, for the sake of your convenience, we have to cancel the 50 bags of Article No. SB356.

    If this trial order proves successful, we will place substantial orders with you.

Sincerely yours,
Roslyn

Step 15

Joanne replies, expressing her appreciation for Roslyn's help to solve the problem and hoping for more business in the future.

To: "Ms. Roslyn Calder"< RoslynCalder@RoslynsEmporium.com>
From: "Ms. Joanne Zhang"< PoseidonTrading@hotmail.com >
Date: March 23, 2016
Subject: Thanks for Your Consideration

Case 2

Abbott Shan from sales department of Good Fortune Trade Company, puts an advertisement on alibaba.com, introducing his company as follows.

Company name: Good Fortune Trade Company

About us: Our company is one of the greatest import and export companies in China . We mainly export electronic and electrical appliances, light industrial products and chemicals. Our imported goods include information technology products, luxury automobiles and cosmetic products.

Contact person: Abbott Shan, Sales Department

Telephone: 86-020-3895689

Address: 165 Zhongshan Road, Yuexiu District, Guangzhou, China

Website: http://www.gftc.com

By chance, Abbott Shan read about Hunter & Co., Ltd. as follows.

Company name: Hunter & Co., Ltd.

Product: Electronic products

Contact person: Lucas Stephan, Overseas Department Manager

Telephone: 0064-4-3895678

Fax: 0064-4-3895679

Address: 320 Royal Parades, Wellington, New Zealand

Then, Abbott Shan writes a letter of inquiry to Hunter & Co., Ltd. Thus, in order to succeed in trading with each other, Abbott Shan and Lucas Stephan exchange correspondence.

Step 1

Abbott Shan makes an inquiry to Hunter & Co., Ltd.

March 20, 2016 **From:** Abbott Shan **To:** Hunter & Co., Ltd.
Dear Sirs, 　　From the Chamber of Commerce of Beijing, we have learned your firm. We take the pleasure of addressing this letter in hope of establishing direct business relations with you. 　　Our company is one of the greatest import and export companies in China and has wide experience in all the lines we handle. We mainly export electronic and electrical appliances, light industrial products and chemicals. 　　Our imported goods include information technology products, luxury automobiles and cosmetic products.

We are looking forward to a productive trade between us.

Yours faithfully,
Abbott Shan
Sales Department

Step 2

Upon receiving the letter, Lucas Stephan, makes a reply, expressing his willingness to enter into a business relationship, making a brief self-introduction, asking for some information and material.

March 21, 2016
From: Lucas Stephan
To: Abbott Shan

Step 3

Now, Abbott Shan gives a reply.

March 22, 2016
From: Abbott Shan
To: Lucas Stephan

Dear Lucas,

    Thank you for your letter of March 21 of your willingness to trade with us.

    Please read the attached files for specific information required in your last letter. Also attached you will find our latest catalogue and price list.

    We usually accept irrevocable sight L/C.

    We hope to receive your reply soon.

Yours faithfully,
Abbott Shan

Step 4

Lucas Stephan asks Abbott to make him an offer, showing his interest in Model No. 0369, Model No. 0370 and Item No. 0381, Item No. 0382, and Item No. 0383.

March 23, 2016
From: Lucas Stephan
To: Abbott Shan

Step 5

Now, Abbott Shan makes an offer.

March 24, 2016 **From:** Abbott Shan **To:** Lucas Stephan

Dear Lucas,
    Thank you for your letter of this morning of your interest in our electronic products.
    We are in a position to supply electronic products in various models and functions. We are pleased to make you an offer as follows.
    Price: Model No. 0369, USD12/set; Model No. 0370, USD12.8/set
           Item No. 0381, USD10/piece; Item No. 0382, USD10/piece and Item No. 0383, USD10.5/piece
    FOB Guangzhou
    Payment: by irrevocable confirmed sight L/C
    Discount: 3% for the total amount of USD5,000, another 0.5% for every USD1,000 more, with 10% as the highest, no discount for a total amount less than USD5,000
    Shipment: within one month after order confirmed
    Validity: one week from the date quoted
    We hope the above terms and conditions become the basis of our future business.
    Looking forward to receiving your order early.
 	
                                                          Sincerely yours,
                                                           Abbott Shan

Step 6

After receiving the offer, Lucas replies immediately, placing an order.

March 25, 2016 **From:** Lucas Stephan **To:** Abbott Shan

Step 7
Abbott confirms receipt of the order.

March 26, 2016
From: Abbott Shan
To: Lucas Stephan

Dear Lucas,

    We are pleased to receive your order. It is almost ready for shipment. Please arrange the payment and open the relevant L/C timely so as to avoid any delay in shipment.

    Thanks.

Sincerely yours,
Abbott Shan

Step 8
Lucas opens the L/C as required and gives Abbott a notice.

March 27, 2016
From: Lucas Stephan
To: Abbott Shan

Step 9

Having learned the information from Abbott that the L/C has reached the Bank of China, Guangzhou Branch, Lucas writes to Abbott, giving him details concerning shipping vessel.

April 5, 2016 **From:** Lucas Stephan **To:** Abbott Shan

Dear Abbott,
  We are glad to learn that the L/C has reached you. Please be noted that we have authorized AIRNET INTERNATIONAL LOGISTICS CO., LTD. for the transportation of the order. Details are as follows.
  Ocean vessel voy. No. : Princess, OSC 3289
  Port of loading: Guangzhou
  Laytime: weather working days of 24 hours, from April 10 to 15
  ETD: April 16
  Please make necessary arrangement for shipment.
 	
                      Sincerely,
                        Lucas

Step 10

As soon as the order is delivered, Abbott writes to Lucas, informing him the detailed shipment information and dispatching transportation documents.

April 14, 2016 **From:** Abbott Shan **To:** Lucas Stephan

Dear Lucas,
  We are glad to tell you that your order No. EP5398 has been shipped on board S.S. Princess as required, which is scheduled to sail for Guangzhou on April 16.
  The relevant shipping documents are enclosed herewith. Please check.
  As agreed, we will draw upon you a sight draft. Please honor it.
  We look forward to your further orders.
 	
                      Yours sincerely,
                       Abbott Shan

Step 11

A month later, Lucas takes delivery of the goods and writes to Abbott, expecting to have further deals.

May 20, 2016   **From:** Lucas Stephan   **To:** Abbott Shan

Case 3

Alisa, sales manager of Nanjing Textile Import & Export Co., Ltd., releases profile information of her company online as follows, in the hope of establishing business relationship with overseas buyers.

Company name: Nanjing Textile Import & Export Co., Ltd.
Address: 77, North Yunnan Road, Nanjing, China
Telephone: 025-83305588
E-mail: nantex@nantex.com.cn
Website: http://www.nantex.com.cn
Brief introduction: Nanjing Textile Import & Export Co., Ltd. established in 1978, and now we are a leading company specializing in textiles and garments manufacturing and exporting. Our products range from textiles, garments and toys. And our department, Garment Dept. 2, has more than 20 years' experience in cooperation with European, USA, Canadian and Australian clients. We are in a position to accept orders against customers' samples, specifying designs and packing requirements. We are also prepared to accept orders with customers own trademarks and brand names. And our strong items are jackets, skiwear, activewear, pants, jeans, children wear, ect.

Nicola Alu, general manager of Nenon International Garments & Textiles, makes an advertisement as follows on alibaba.com, hoping to purchase textile products.

Company name: Nenon International Garments & Textiles

About us: We are the importer of all kinds of garments/textiles, such as T-shirts, polo shirts, jeans, all kinds of ladies wear, all kinds of children's wear, bed sheets, etc. So we are looking for standard manufacturers and exporters of the above mentioned products to have a business transaction.

Contact person: Mr. Nicola Alu, General Manager

E-mail: nigt@nigt.com.cn

Telephone: 684-228-9226604

Fax: 684-228-2218125

Step 1 Inquiry

Alisa writes an inquiry to Mr. Nicola Alu, making a brief self-introduction of her company, in the hope of establishing business relationship with this overseas buyer.

From:
To:
Date:
Subject:

Step 2 Reply to the Inquiry

Nicola Alu receives the E-mail from Alisa and replies to express his willingness to establish business relations, showing interest in textiles and garments, inviting an offer and asking for the latest price lists and catalogues.

| From: |
| To: |
| Date: |
| Subject: |

Step 3 An Offer

Upon getting the reply from Nicola Alu, Alisa sends an E-mail back immediately, making an offer to Mr. Nicola Alu, giving payment requirement—confirmed, irrevocable letter of credit, proving the information and material needed.

From:
To:
Date:
Subject:

Step 4 Counter-offer

Upon receipt of the offer from Alisa, Nicola Alu makes a counter-offer, considering the price on the high side, asking for a 15% discount for a total purchase of USD10,000, confirming a 60-day confirmed, irrevocable letter of credit for terms of payment.

From:
To:
Date:
Subject:

Step 5 A Firm Offer

Following Alu's counter-offer, Alisa makes a firm offer subject to reply within one week—Price: as shown in the price list, for a 15% discount; Total amount: at least USD10,000; Payment: confirmed, irrevocable letter of credit payable by draft at sight to be opened 30 days before the time of shipment; Shipment: within 30 days after receipt of the relevant L/C.

From:
To:
Date:
Subject:

Step 6 Order

Nicola Alu accepts the offer and places an order.

QNTY	Item No.	Description	Unit Price
500	CW121	Cotton	USD6 FOB Nanjing
500	CW122	Cotton	USD8 FOB Nanjing
1,000	PS108	Silk	USD25 FOB Nanjing
1,000	PS109	Cotton	USD20 FOB Nanjing
1,000	JW209	Cotton	USD15 FOB Nanjing
1,000	TS202	Cotton	USD15 FOB Nanjing
1,000	TS203	Silk	USD20 FOB Nanjing

All the other terms should be applicable as agreed.

From:
To:
Date:
Subject:

Step 7 Order Acknowledgment

Alisa loses no time to acknowledge the order with expression of thanks, assuring Alu of prompt and careful execution of order, expressing her desire for future orders, restating the key contents of the order, the shipping instructions, the terms of payment and attaching catalogues of other products likely to be of interest and a sales confirmation in duplicate for counter-signature.

| **From:** |
| **To:** |
| **Date:** |
| **Subject:** |
| |

Step 8 Urging the Establishment of L/C

Two weeks after acknowledging the order, Alisa still has not received any information about the opening of the L/C from Nicola Alu, she writes an E-mail to urge the establishment of the L/C.

From:
To:
Date:
Subject:

Step 9 Informing the Establishment of L/C

Nicola Alu replies to Alisa, explaining the reasons for delaying of the L/C, informing her of the details of the relevant L/C, such as L/C No., amount, opening date, opening bank, advising bank, etc.

From:
To:
Date:
Subject:

Step 10 L/C Amendment & Extension

Alisa receives the L/C, finding some discrepancies concerning terms of payment and the total amount. So, she writes to Nicola Alu immediately, requiring the L/C to be amended by cable accordingly soon, and the shipment date and L/C expiry date to be extended.

From:
To:
Date:
Subject:

Step 11 Giving Shipping Instructions and Packing Requirements

After receiving Alisa's confirmation of the L/C amendment, Nicola Alu writes to Alisa, giving shipping instructions, shipping mark and packing requirements: each in an inner box and 10 boxes in an export carton, lined with waterproof plastic sheet.

From:
To:
Date:
Subject:

Step 12 Giving Shipping Advice and Dispatching Shipping Documents

Alisa, having gotten Alu's shipping instructions and packing requirements, makes arrangement of the shipping of the order immediately. Then she gives Alu shipping advice: ETD and ETA, name of the vessel and shipping mark, asking Alu to cover the order for insurance. She also dispatches the shipping documents, asking for acceptance of the 30-day draft.

From: **To:**   **Date:**   **Subject:**

Step 13 Sending Information about Insurance Coverage

Nicola Alu receives the details of shipment from Alisa and arranges insurance immediately. Then he replies, informing Alisa of the insurance coverage of the order.

From:
To:
Date:
Subject:

Step 14 Complaint

Nicola Alu takes delivery of the goods. But on unpacking, he finds some errors: for Item No. TS203, the 1,000 articles are cotton not silk. He writes to Alisa, requiring her to reship the goods needed soon, also asking how to deal with the wrongly-delivered T-shirts.

From: **To:**   **Date:**   **Subject:**

Chapter 17　Business Correspondence　　235

Step 15　Reply to the Complaint

Alisa replies to apologize and proposes ways to solve the problems, ensuring him to avoid such mistakes, promising to offer special allowance.

From:
To:
Date:
Subject:

Step 16 Acceptance of the Complaint Settlement

Nicola Alu receives Alisa's reply and accepts her settlement on the condition that a 5% percent discount should be offered.

| From: |
| To: |
| Date: |
| Subject: |
| |

Chapter 17 Business Correspondence

Step 17 Settlement of the Complaint

Alisa replies to accept Alu's requirement, providing more information about the latest products, hoping for more business between each other, ensuring Alu to fulfill the future order accurately.

From:
To:
Date:
Subject:

2. Internal Correspondence

Internal correspondence refers to the correspondence within an organization or institution. E-mail, as a major form of internal correspondence, covers all sorts of business affairs involved in a factory or a company. Comparatively speaking, internal E-mails, which are mainly to colleagues, can be not as formal as the external correspondence. The signature can just include the sender's name and/or position. The company's name, address, telephone number, if not necessary, can be omitted.

Bear in mind the principles, guidelines and tips for writing business E-mails, and start practicing.

1) A Newcomer's Internal Correspondence

E-mail Writing 1

Situation: After having graduated from a university, you work in the sales department in a joint venture in China selling projectors and other electric products to other countries. As a newcomer, you need to be familiar with the products of your company.

Write an E-mail to the production manager Paul Liu expressing your wish to visit the production base.

(1) Telling your purpose.

(2) Seeking for help.

(3) Expressing thanks.

E-mail Writing 2

Situation: In the first month, you were unable to develop any new client and get any order.

Write an E-mail to the sales manager Peter Davis.

(1) Apologizing for not doing well.

(2) Summarizing the possible reasons.

(3) Saying what you will do to improve.

E-mail Writing 3

Situation: With your painstaking efforts, you have managed to get an Egyptian company to show interest in the projectors manufactured by your company. You feel very happy, but you are not sure about what to do next.

Write an E-mail to the sales manager Peter Davis for help.

(1) Telling him the good news.

(2) Expressing your puzzles.

(3) Expressing your wish for his help.

E-mail Writing 4

How would the sales manager reply to the above E-mail? Write an E-mail.

E-mail Writing 5

Situation: Before deciding to buy your products, Sarah Edwards, the sales manager of that Egyptian company had made an appointment to visit your company.

But the schedule had to be changed due to some unforeseeable circumstance. She wrote an E-mail to your sales manager Peter Davis. The following is her E-mail.

To: Peter Davis
From: Sarah Edwards
Subject: A Change in Schedule

Dear Mr. Davis,

 I am sorry to tell you that I need to reschedule our factory visit.

 I have just received word that our company's annual board meeting will be scheduled for the exact dates of our travel and my attendance at the meeting is mandatory. If possible, I would like to reschedule our visit by the end of June or beginning of July.

 Please let me know if these dates would work for you. Again I am sorry for the last minute change of plans and the inconvenience it might cause you.

Best regards
Sarah Edwards
Sales Manager

Writing directions: The sales manager Peter Davis is so busy that he asks you to write an E-mail in the name of him in reply to Sarah Edwards' E-mail, feeling sorry and suggesting other dates. He reminds you to send the E-mail to him after finishing it. Now, write an E-mail in the name of sales manager Peter Davis to Sarah Edwards.

E-mail Writing 6

Situation: With the help of the sales manager Peter Davis, you recently won an order of 30 projectors from that Egyptian company.

Write an E-mail to him and express thanks for his help.

E-mail Writing 7

Write an E-mail to the production manager Paul Liu to enquire the progress of production against the order.

2) Colleagues' Internal Correspondence

E-mail Writing 1

Writing directions: You are the sales manager Peter Davis. You write an E-mail to Lili Nuttle in the purchasing department in charge for additional office supplies.

In the following E-mail, the first and the last sentences have been written down. You need to complete the information of "From:" and "Date:", tell the reason why the sales department needs additional office supplies, and list what office supplies your department needs.

> **To:** Purchasing Department
> **ATTN:** Lili Nuttle
> **From:**
> **Date:**
> **Subject:** Office Supply Shortage
>
> Dear Ms. Nuttle,
>   I am writing to request that additional office supplies be purchased and supplied for the sales department.
>   Thank you for your attention to this matter. Everyone in the sales department would greatly appreciate it!
>
> Yours sincerely,

E-mail Writing 2

Situation: You are the HR manager for an international company. Recently you have received a memo announcing that Bob Justlin is appointed financial director of your company. You have heard of him, but you don't know him very much.

Write an E-mail to him, expressing your warm welcome to him.

E-mail Writing 3

Situation: You are a regional sales manager for an international company. You have been asked to go to a meeting at your company's head office. You cannot go, so somebody else will go in your place.

Write an E-mail to Daniel Long, who is organizing the meeting.

(1) Apologizing for not being able to go to the meeting.

(2) Explaining why you cannot go.

(3) Saying who will go.

E-mail Writing 4

Situation: You are the HR manager for an international company. Recently you have received a letter from one of your employees, Andy Lee, who is seeking the opportunity of working abroad. For some reasons his request cannot be met.

Write an E-mail to him in reply to his letter.

(1) Telling him you have received his letter.

(2) Showing your acknowledgement to his good performance in work.

(3) Explaining why his request cannot be met.

E-mail Writing 5

Situation: You are the sales manager, and you want to meet production manager to talk about the large order you just received.

Write an E-mail to the production manager.

(1) Telling him about the large order.

(2) Saying what you would like him to do about this.

(3) Explaining why it is urgent.

E-mail Writing 6

Situation 1: Here is an E-mail to require all staff of sales department attend the sales meeting.

To: All staff of sales department
From: Peter Davis
Subject: Sales Meeting

Dear all,

    Please clear your schedules to attend our monthly sales review meeting next Tuesday afternoon at 2 P.M. at the conference room.

    Each sales staff will be required to give a report for 5-10 minutes of current accounts and sales numbers. The meeting is scheduled to last 2 hours, so please be prepared to attend for the entire afternoon. Any absence or partial absence must be cleared by the human resources department by Friday at the last. Attendance is mandatory, no exceptions.

                                                     Best regards

                                                     Peter Davis

---

Situation 2: You are one of the staff members of sales department. After reading the notice of sales meeting several days ago, you have prepared a report and been ready for the meeting. But on Wednesday this week, you are asked to go on business in another city for five days and will be unable to attend it.

Writing directions: Write an E-mail to sales manager Peter Davis to ask for a leave.

(1) Apologizing for your absence from the scheduled meeting.

(2) Stating your reasons(remember to mention the name of the city).

(3) Suggesting another colleague read the report for you.

(4) Apologizing again.

E-mail Writing 7

Situation: You are the general manager Samuel Johnson, and you want to meet your production manager Paul Liu this week.

Please write an E-mail to him.

(1) Telling him when you would like to meet him.

(2) Why you would like to meet him.

(3) Where you can meet him.

E-mail Writing 8

Situation: The general manager Samuel Johnson wrote an E-mail to the production manager Paul Liu to talk about production costs. Here is his E-mail.

> **To:** Paul Liu
> **From:** Samuel Johnson
> **Subject:** Production Costs
>
> Dear Paul,
>   According to our latest sales numbers, we are doing very well. We've seen our sales more than quadruple over the last 6 months alone. But even though these numbers should have tickled pink, we still have a major problem.
>   Because of material shortages worldwide, the cost of production has shot up over tenfold. So instead of a healthy margin of profit, we are walking a fine line between profitability and non-profitability. Can you help me to brainstorm what some solutions to this problem may be?
>   Thanks!
>
>   Samuel

Writing directions: You are the production manager. You write an E-mail in reply to the general manager's E-mail.

(1) The way of reducing production costs: finding a new supplier for raw materials.

(2) Reason: previous supplier kept raising the prices of raw materials; result: smaller margin of profit.

(3) Showing confidence.

Chapter 18

Business Memo Writing

You are a supervisor of the marketing department of your company. You realize that your staffing needs have increased due to the changes in the latest 2 years due to many different causes. Write a memo to the director of your company requesting more funds to safeguard a stable labor force in your department and increase sales.

Pre-write: Answer questions of "who" "what" "when" "why" "where" and "how".
_____
_____

During writing: Draft the memo using the correct memo format and checklist.
_____
_____
_____
_____
_____
_____
_____

Re-write: Check for errors, flow and tone.
_____
_____
_____
_____

244　实用商务英语写作

Chapter 19

Business Report Writing

Case 1

You and your friends decide to start your own business while in the university. After discussion, you agree to run an on-line supermarket, which provides fine quality daily necessities for residents nearby. You decide to conduct a market research and make a report for further business discussion.

Your market research campaign will follow in steps.

Step 1 Decide the Purpose of Your Report

The purpose of the report will be identifying how many competitors nearby. _____
_____
_____
_____
_____

Step 2 Discuss about Research Method

What kind of method can be used to approach targeted purpose? Or by what means can you gather information?

1. Sending out questionnaire
2. _____
3. _____
4. _____
5. _____

Step 3 Discuss for More Details of Market Research

1. How much time do you have for the research?
_____
_____

2. How many people do you need to fulfill the research?
_____
_____

3. When and where will you carry out the survey and by what means?
_____
_____

4. Is there any potential difficulty in the survey?
_____
_____

Step 4 Questionnaire Design

Your group decides to carry out the market research by sending out questionnaires. Now please discuss and note down the following topics.

1. What is the purpose of the questionnaire?
_____
_____

2. What sections may be included in the questionnaire?
_____
_____

Step 5 Result Analysis

After you gather the returned questionnaire, you need to analyze the data, based on which your report will be built.

The data should be noted down in a table similar to the following example.

No.	A	B	C	D	Remarks
1	4	16	0	10	
2	11	0	0	5	Others
3	0	30	0	0	
4	21	4	0	5	
5	5	12	1	12	

By filling such table, you will develop a clearer understanding of the responses. Then, based on the questions that you offered in the questionnaire and the responses, you will develop a report about the local market that you target at.

Step 6 Team Division

You need to allocate the writing mission among your group members. Each person is responsible for a certain section. Set a deadline for writing and editing.

Case 2

Please prepare a formal report on a topic such as the followings (approximate length: 6 to 15 pages of text, plus front and back matter).

1. A business problem based on case information and involving research.

2. The feasibility of selecting a site for a new manufacturing/entertainment facility.

3. A program on PC in campus.

Chapter 20

Business Proposal Writing

After you have finished the market research and written a report, you need to discuss and finish a business proposal. This proposal will be the result of your brainstorming and the foundation for future actions. And this proposal will be submitted to investors that have interests in venture.

You need to accomplish this mission by following steps.

Step 1 Overview of Your Research Report

Section 1 Local Competitor

1. Is there any local competitor nearby?
   _____
   _____

2. What are the advantages and disadvantages of the competitors?
   _____
   _____

Section 2 Local Consumer

3. What are the features of local consumer?
   _____
   _____

4. Is there any conventional way of consumption locally?
   _____
   _____

5. Is there any brand loyalty or brand preference among local consumers?
   _____
   _____

6. Is there any vacuum market locally?
   _____
   _____

Step 2 Develop Your Own Business Idea

1. The main business is _____

2. The supermarket offers a range of products including:
_____
_____

3. The differences between you and your competitors:
_____
_____

4. The source of products may include:
_____
_____

5. The competitive edge in terms of sources is:
_____
_____

6. The sales method will be:
_____
_____

7. The competitive edge in terms of sales method is:
_____
_____

8. The after sales service include:
_____
_____

Step 3 Making Proposals

You need to discuss about how to start your business. The discussion may be divided into a short-term plan (3 months) and a long-term plan (3 years). Your plan should be presented in a numbered list.

After you figure out the business plan, please elaborate the benefits of your proposal. The benefits will be the compelling evidence to persuade the reader. Also, the benefits can be presented in a single paragraph, or a numbered list.

Step 4 Coping with Financial Problem

You need to develop a budget plan for starting the business. The budget should include the expenses on office facilities (if any), personnel, distribution network, sales promotion, etc. An example will be as follows. You can fill in the blank according to your discussion.

Item	Number	Unit Price	Total

Besides the budget, you also need to develop a financial plan for the near 1-3 years, in order to highlight the feasibility of your proposal. An example of the financial plan is as follows. You can fill in the blank according to your discussion.

Period of time	Target of Business	Expenses	Revenue

Step 5 Writing the Proposal

With the information you've gathered, you can begin to write the proposal now. After you finish the writing, please remember to refine it by editing.

参考文献

[1] 安锦兰，李文洁. 商务英语写作. 北京：清华大学出版社，2014.
[2] 曹菱. 商务英语信函. 北京：外语教学与研究出版社，2000.
[3] 陈良璇. 商务英语函件与单证. 郑州：河南人民出版社，2004.
[4] 陈庆勋，耿纪永，程浩东. 英语应用文写作大全. 北京：社会科学文献出版社，2003.
[5] 程同春. 新编国际商务英语函电. 南京：东南大学出版社，2001.
[6] 何虹. 商务英语写作. 2版. 武汉：武汉大学出版社，2012.
[7] 胡亦武. 实用商务英语写作. 广州：华南理工大学出版社，2003.
[8] 黄玛莉. 现代商务英文写作. 北京：世界图书出版社，2004.
[9] 戚云方. 新编外经贸英语函电与谈判. 杭州：浙江大学出版社，2005.
[10] 施晓燕，李红. 商务英语应用文写作. 北京：科学出版社，2010.
[11] 王兴孙. 新编进出口英语函电. 上海：上海交通大学出版社，2001.
[12] 王玉. 高级商务英语写作. 北京：外语教学与研究出版社，2014.
[13] 杨伶俐. 商务英语写作教程. 2版. 北京：中国人民大学出版社，2014.
[14] 叶兴国，王光林. 高级商务英语写作. 北京：外语教学与研究出版社，2014
[15] 诸葛霖. 外贸业务英文函电. 北京：对外经济贸易大学出版社，2003.